LOCOMOTION PAPERS NUMBER ON

SOUTHERN RAILWAY HALTS

SURVEY AND GAZETTEER

by

R.W. Kidner

THE OAKWOOD PRESS

ISBN 0 85361 321 4

Printed by S&S Press, Abingdon, Oxford

A postcard view of High Rocks Halt near Tunbridge Wells about 1907; note the heavily staggered platforms. *Robson, Tunbridge Wells*

Published by
The OAKWOOD PRESS
P.O. Box 122, Headington, Oxford

SOUTHERN RAILWAY HALTS

Contents

Hurst Green Halt as opened in 1907, with railmotor train from Oxted entering. The halt was later rebuilt and extended, and closed in 1961 when a station was opened on the other side of the bridge. *Author's Collection*

One of the thirteen LSWR 'H13' class steamcars which worked many halt services from 1905. *Lens of Sutton*

SECR steamcar No. 1 at Three Oaks Bridge Halt about 1907. *Author's Collection*

Southern Railway Halts

Introduction

Fifteen years ago the title 'Halt' disappeared from the Southern Region time-tables, and the thirty or so halts which had survived from the 150 originally constructed became stations. Today, when so many stations are simply platforms for trains to stop at, it may be necessary to recall why halts had to be invented. At the turn of the century, most stations were places of comfort. They offered 1st and 3rd class waiting rooms with fires, parcels and telegraph offices, clean lavatories, bookstalls; porters to carry luggage, shunters to attach horse-boxes and station masters to apologise for any late running. Clearly not all villages could provide enough passengers for such establishments. The railway companies had seen the tramways reaching out from the towns, offering waiting passengers no shelter; from 1903 motor buses began to do the same. Co-incidentally, the steam railcar which had not succeeded in earlier experiments, was being re-invented. The two together, halt and railcar, could offer a new dimension in economical transport. A short wooden platform, unstaffed, and a steamcar consuming little coal – what could be better?

So in the flush of enthusiasm before the motor buses bit deep into suburban and rural transport, about eighty halts were put up by the constituent companies of the later Southern Railway. Many are long gone, as are most of the seventy put up later. That so many are now totally forgotten is the reason for this book. However, there is one other factor: as research proceeded a surprising discovery was made that not all sources agreed as to which stops had been halts, and this survey attempts to sort out such confusions, as well as to locate and describe halts both forgotten and surviving. Any reader who cannot straight away remember where Albert Road Halt and Albert Road Bridge Halt were, will, it is hoped, find it useful and interesting.

R.W. Kidner 1985

Bell Punch Company, London.

SOUTHERN & G.W. RLYS.
RAIL MOTOR CAR. 3rd Cl.

This Ticket must be punched in the Section to which the Passenger is entitled to travel and must be shown on demand. This Ticket is not transferable and is issued subject to the Bye-laws, Regulations and Conditions published in the Companies' Bills and Notices.

Sandsfoot Castle Halt | Melcombe Regis

Fare 2½d

C 6342

Harty Road Halt, one of two built in 1905 on the Sheppey branch; in common with other SECR halts at the time, it does not carry the word 'Halt' on its nameboard. *Lens of Sutton*

Typical of the LBSCR early halts; this is Nutbourne, looking west. The notice is headed 'Motor Car Halt'. *Lens of Sutton*

Chapter One

What was a 'Halt'?

There had always been a few crude platforms put up for special, usually non-public, purposes, for example, the single platform on the down line near Farningham Road erected in 1870 for the Horton Kirby Boys Home.

If these were given names at all, they were referred to as 'platforms'. The term 'halt' came with the rail-motor boom of 1903–10. It was to be a simple wooden platform without signals, staff or shelter, one-coach long – something to counter the existing tramcar competition and the approaching motor-bus challenge, by providing more closely-spaced stops and hopefully more frequent 'trains'. Tickets would be issued by a conductor-guard. There was the problem of lighting; if a halt was near a guarded crossing or a siding, that was all right; if not, then it would be open in daylight hours only.

This was how it started; but soon halts were being put up which were not on motor-served lines, some requiring ticket offices. By popular demand shelters had to be provided. Later some 'demoted' stations joined the ranks. The parameters of what was a halt and what a station were never clear-cut. For example, North Hayling station was crude, unstaffed and lonely, but it was opened in 1867 and was always a 'station' – if it had been put up after 1903 it would have been a halt. The fact is that there was always some uncertainty about the classification. Not all halts carried the word on their name-boards at first, and many disappeared without being photographed or recorded by enthusiasts. How then can we be sure?

There were three obvious sources – time-tables, the Railway Clearing House Handbook of Stations (RCH), and Ordnance Survey Maps. However, the RCH dubs more halts than Bradshaw does. Maps should be reliable; there was good reason, especially for the Bartholomew half-inch version, for maps to be clear; no country walker should arrive hot-foot at a halt to send a telegram or use the lavatory. An experienced walker in due course would be well aware what the note 'halt' on the map meant; that at some, all trains stopped; at others waving arms were required. A few (not on the SR) were subject to such esoteric rules as 'Down trains will stop on notice being given to the guard of the previous up train'. But the maps did not always agree with the RCH or Bradshaw. For example, on the East Kent Railway Bradshaw for some reason gave Poison Cross as the only halt, though there were several other platforms equally wretched and unused. To the map-makers, the only halt on the line was Ash Town!

There are two secondary sources: Clinker's 'Register of Closed Stations' and Clark's *Southern Region Chronology and Record*. But, not surprisingly, they do not always agree with each other on halts, nor with the above sources. The difficulty in being sure whether a station was a halt or not, in retrospect, can be exemplified by the situation on the Callington branch. Latchley and Chilsworthy were both marked as halts on the OS maps, and appear so in The Railway Clearing House Handbook of Stations, but Bradshaw, Clark and Clinker all regard them as stations. A book on the PDSWJR gives Latchley as a station and Chilsworthy as a halt. An LSWR official, writing about the line just before it opened, made it clear that Latchley was a 'Halte' (a spelling then used), the only one on the branch, as Seven Stones and Chilsworthy were later additions. He quotes the platform length as 256 ft, 12 ft longer than that at the main station of Gunnislake, and it was manned, so why it alone was a halt is unclear.

To make this work complete, we have included any 'halt' given by one or more of the sources mentioned; but we have not had regard to local reports, for they tended to refer to any one-platform station as 'the halt'.

The new halts were known as 'railmotor halts'; the word motor at this time did not only refer to petrol cars, which were mostly called automobiles, but to anything with an engine in it. By extension, the push-pulls were also called railmotors. It may be that the railway companies felt that by using the word motor they were stealing some of the thunder of the petrol buses which were now spluttering around a few cities. In their time-tables, the LSW usually headed a railmotor working by the word Car. There is no doubt that it was seen as a new era in transport; the journal *Motor Transport* drew attention to the fact that 100 cars a day would be running to St Budeaux, 60 on the GWR and 40 on the LSWR. Some claims were exaggerated; the Dick Kerr petrol cars on the LBSC were said to be capable of 55 mph – somewhat frightening when they were considered by the GNR, who had one, to be too uncomfortable for passenger use even at low speeds.

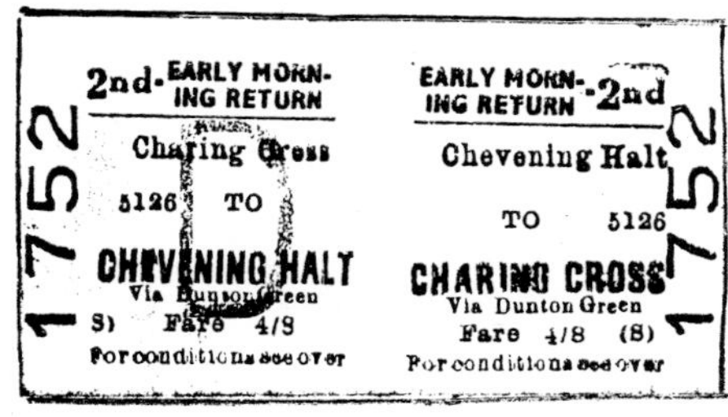

Chapter Two

Early Enthusiasm: 1903–10

The first dip into the unknown waters of steamcar operation was made in 1902 by Dugald Drummond of the LSWR, but the car did not go into service at once, being loaned to the GWR for trials. In June 1903 the first two cars (one owned by the LBSC) started work on the joint LSW/LBSC Southsea branch. It was a thorough attempt to use steamcars as tramcars. The double-line branch was singled and even the terminus was abolished and replaced by a halt platform nearby. Two halts (Albert Road Bridge and Jessie Road) were added on a branch not much over a mile long, and conductors with Bell Punch ticket racks travelled in the car. There was one every 20 minutes. It was not a success; there were mechanical troubles and problems with parcels and through tickets, and it only lasted until 1914. However, two somewhat improved steamcars were built which worked on the Basingstoke & Alton Light Railway and elsewhere. In 1905 an even better design came out, of which 13 were built bringing steamcar services to many parts of the system. A number of 'suburban' halts were built, such as Meyrick Park between Bournemouth West and Central stations (with a fare of only 1*d*. from the halt to West). Three were built just outside Exeter on the Honiton line (Lions Holt, Mount Pleasant Road, Whipton Bridge). Another suburban service was that from Devonport to St Budeaux, for which halts were put up at Albert Road, near Ford, and at Camels Head and Weston Mill at St Budeaux.

The LSWR made a great fuss about the institution of this service, probably because it was in direct competition with a similar GWR service. It seems to have had its problems; in September 1906 the directors of the Plymouth, Devonport & South Western Railway, who owned the line, complained that they had put up the halts but the motor cars were not available; the steamcars to serve the line were to be provided by the LSWR. The halts were officially opened on 1st November, 1906; however, according to *Motor Transport*, at least one car was working by the end of September. This service was later extended back to Plymouth Friary, remaining motor-worked long after the steamcars had gone, with 'O2' or 'M7' tanks attached to 2-car push-pull sets made up from steamcar bodies.

The LBSCR began its railcar-cum-halt programme with the purchase in February 1905 of two Dick Kerr 4-wheel petrol cars; these were put on the Eastbourne–St Leonards run, and halts were opened at Stone Cross, Pevensey Bay, Pevensey Sluice (Normans Bay), Cooden Golf, Glyne Gap and Collington Wood. However, the cars proved unable to take the traffic offering, and they were replaced by two

Aldrington Halt near Hove in 1933, showing the Sentinel steamcar No. 6 which worked the Dyke Branch. *H.C. Casserley*

Bandon Halt near Wallington, opened in 1906 but closed as early as 1914; the 'Terrier-cum-Balloon' motor is trailing a six-wheeled coach. *Lens of Sutton*

steamcars. The petrol cars went to the Kemp Town branch, where Lewes Road station was later changed to a halt, and an extra halt added at Hartington Road, opened in June 1906.

At the same time trials were being made with 'Terrier' 0–6–0Ts working with single vestibuled 'Balloon' control trailers, and they began a service from Brighton to Worthing in September 1905, with halts at Holland Road, Dyke Junction, Fishersgate and Ham Bridge. There is also said to have been a halt at the Kingston Goods Station, and in 1910 one was added at Bungalow Town on the west side of the estuary at Shoreham. On a line with its mead of fast traffic, there must have been some worry about these motors doodling along and stopping everywhere. However, they *could* move; a *Railway Magazine* reader logged one – a 'Terrier' temporarily converted to 2–4–0T – covering the run (10½ miles with nine stops) in 26 minutes. No stop took more than 30 seconds, and two halts were cleared in 5 seconds each! It is worth noting that by 1930 the push-pulls were allowed 32 minutes for this trip, with ten stops. Nowadays, the electric trains do it in 24 minutes with only eight stops. Nevertheless, a fast train from London leaving Hove 16 minutes behind the motor would be only 5 minutes behind at Worthing, so the 'locals' had to look smart about it.

In April 1906 a similar service was started at the other end of the West Coast Line, from Portsmouth to Chichester, with new halts at Bedhampton, Warblington (1907), Southbourne, Nutbourne and Fishbourne. By 1907 there were 17 'Balloon' trailers available and their use was extended to other parts of the system. These cars carried conductor-guards and were third-class only.

Horsham also became a rail-motor base, with halts opened on the Crawley line at Rusper Road, Roffey Road, and Lyons Crossing (Ifield). The units worked from a bay at Horsham, combining trips to Three Bridges with darts up to Dorking and sometimes further afield. Another area to benefit was that extending west and south from Tunbridge Wells West, though only three halts were put up, at Monks Lane on the Edenbridge Town line, High Rocks near Tunbridge Wells, and Hurst Green at the junction south of Oxted. These were only 100 ft long and it was never intended that ordinary trains should stop at them. Therefore the service depended entirely on the availability of the motors. When they first opened, in June 1907, only the Horsham motor got as far as Tunbridge Wells, once a day, so that was the service at High Rocks, one train per day each way. It was a bit better later, but even by the 'thirties these halts were not places to go casually for a train; if you missed the lunch-time motor-train at High Rocks or Monks Lane you had a seven-hour wait for the next!

Meanwhile, what was the SECR doing? It had eight steamcars built in 1904/5, the first going on to the Sheppey Light Railway, where extra halts were added at Brambledown and Harty Road (all stations on this line looked like halts, but only these two were so called). However, the most ambitious project related to the Port Victoria service from Gravesend. The Port Victoria pier had attracted little traffic, and it was necessary to develop local traffic in the Isle of Grain, otherwise called the Hundred of Hoo. It was decided to build a string of halts, to be motor-worked. These each served rather differing purposes: Milton Road and Denton were suburban, Milton Ranges for shooting parties – these three were on the North Kent Line before Hoo Junction. Then Uralite was for workers at the British Uralite factory, High Halden was agricultural, being at the existing Wybourne Siding, as was Beluncle, at the Miskin Siding. Middle Stoke seems to have had no particular purpose, being in the bleakest part of the Stoke Marsh. Grain Crossing served a scattered community without proper roads. The halts were cheaply built mostly of old sleepers, and the nameboards did not carry the word Halt. So the steamcars went to work, twelve per day, with a short working to Cliffe and back. However, there was an increasing presence of industry and military on the 'island', and it seems that the 56-seat cars could not take the morning and evening traffic as time went on; sometimes they were run in tandem or with six-wheel trailers. In 1908 they were taken off and a 150-seat rake of vestibuled six-wheelers substituted. After 1914 traffic increased further, and one or two push-pull sets of six-wheelers were used to help out; some trains were run fast to Sharnal Street and then stopped at the halts; one morning train terminated at Uralite. There was also a lot of goods traffic, including military and naval stores; one can imagine the Traffic Department reflecting ruefully that, though there were seven stopping places on the branch, only the two stations had loops – an unstaffed and unsignalled halt on a single line is not much use in an emergency.

For the suburban service between Woodside and Selsdon Road, to be worked turn-about by SECR and LBSC steamcars, halts were put up at Bingham Road and Spencer Road. Hastings–Rye was another motor service, with halts at Three Oaks, Doleham and Snailham; the Westerham branch got a halt at Chevening.

Eight steamcars were not enough, and in 1909/10 eight 'P' class 0–6–0Ts, a poor copy of the 'Terriers', were built to work with control trailers. However, several non-halt services were motor-worked, and the availability of motor-trains remained very thin. Two non-motor vestibuled sets of four-wheelers were made up for guard-conductor services on Sheppey and the Isle of Grain, but for all its remaining life the SECR was short of suitable stock for halt services.

The Isle of Wight Central Railway had one steamcar and one rather odd push-and-pull set, but in the island there were then no halts officially; later several were so recognised.

To close this period there follows a list of 1903–10 halts not mentioned above.

LSWR
On the Bodmin–Wadebridge line, Grogley, Nanstallon, Dunmere; Exmouth line, Polsloe Bridge and Clyst St Mary; at Plymouth, Lucas Terrace; Bishops Waltham branch, Durley; near Fareham, Knowle Asylum; near Honiton, Roundball; Borden branch, Kingsley; on the Portland line, Westham and Wyke Regis (nominally LSW/GW joint). A new halt at Elmore on the Lee-on-Solent branch was called a halt, but the other two equally dreadful existing platforms were not so-called officially until later.

LBSCR
West Croydon–Sutton line, Bandon and Beeches; Seaford branch, Southease; between Ford and Angmering, Lyminster.

SECR
Canterbury–Whitstable line, Blean; between Paddock Wood and Yalding, Beltring; Paddock Wood–Maidstone, Teston Crossing; near Ramsgate, Ebbsfleet. On the Guildford–Reading line, Sandhurst and Sindlesham; on the Dartford–Gravesend line, Stone Crossing and Swanscombe; Cheriton near Shorncliffe; and Folkestone Warren, a halt which became notorious by being moved 160 ft nearer the sea by a landslide in 1915.

The Lynton and Barnstaple narrow gauge line also had three 'platforms', at Pilton, Snapper and Parracombe, but they do not seem to have been called halts at the time.

Ebbsfleet & Cliffsend Halt, near Ramsgate, about 1910 with a main-line train headed by 'D' class No. 75 passing. *Lens of Sutton*

Warren Halt near Folkestone, with a railmotor entering; this halt was moved bodily 160 ft nearer the sea by the famous 1915 landslide. *Author's Collection*

Beluncle Halt, another SECR 1906 opening, on the Port Victoria line; although photographed in 1932, the nameboard still reads only 'Beluncle'. *Author's Collection*

Chapter Three

A Dull Period: 1911–23

After the first enthusiasm for halts died down, almost the only new ones put up for more than a decade were for working people of various sorts. There were halts for the Army at Westcott Ranges near Gomshall, Woodsford near Dorchester, and at Richborough Castle near Sandwich. Munition workers got Church Manorway on the North Kent line (which actually had cross-overs for London trains terminating, but only lasted three years) and Crow Park near Swanwick. Lake Halt near Hamworthy was for shipbuilders, Mountfield on the Hastings line for gypsum miners, Chislet and Snowdown for coal-miners, Salfords on the Brighton line for the Monotype Works. For golfers halts were opened at Bramshot on the LSW main line and Caffyns on the narrow-gauge Lynton & Barnstaple (though this may have been there a few years before public opening in 1916). The only halts for local purposes were at Longfield on the Gravesend West line, East Malling, South Street and Tankerton on the Whitstable Harbour branch, Lyghe on the Redhill–Tonbridge line, Stonehall in East Kent and Reedham near Purley.

One curious event occurred in December 1922, when a steamer hit the pier of the Kings Ferry Bridge over the Swale in Sheppey. Because the rail bridge was out of action for a year, it was necessary to open to the public the staff Kings Ferry Bridge Halt on the south side of the river, and to set up a very temporary halt on the north side, so that by running trains from both sides up to the river, some communication would be kept going. The south side halt kept going after service was restored on 1st November, 1923; it was renamed Swale Halt in 1929.

Meanwhile all the companies had become disenchanted with steamcars. The LBSC dropped their two around 1911; the LSW began to experiment with 2–2–0T and later 0–4–0T engines hauling control trailers, but they were not the answer and standard 0–4–4Ts took over. From 1916 the steamcars were withdrawn and converted to trailer sets, and at the same time some more push-pull sets were made up by breaking the 4-coach 'bogie block' sets into pairs. The SECR kept most of their cars going until war economies shut some services on which they worked; they fitted out seven sets of three six-wheelers in 1914, also a few years later fitted a few 'R'/'Rl' 0–4–4Ts for motor working, but many halt lines reverted to normal trains. The LBSC built a number of push-and-pull sets with side-corridors, and also added extra coaches to the previously single 'Balloon' trailers. By 1922 the LBSC had 24 push-pull sets, all vestibuled; the LSW also 24, 14 vestibuled, and the SECR 9, or possibly 11, none vestibuled.

Southbourne Halt. *Lens of Sutton*

Hardley Halt, built by British Rail in 1958 for workmen on the Fawley line, lasted only seven years. *Lens of Sutton*

Chapter Four

The Southern Railway: 1923–48

By the time of Grouping, a few halts had been closed by war economies or other reasons, but the new Southern Railway clearly approved of the idea, since it opened twenty new halts over the years, and went in for a strong rebuilding programme. Early in its life the SR had started to use pre-cast concrete, and the halt was a good medium for trying out the new skills. The result was not very attractive, except when new, but the material was durable and needed no paint. Almost all the old wooden halts were so treated over a period, usually being lengthened at the same time. Standard lamp poles were used and, since many halts were now surrounded with electricity, some were bathed in light, so unlike the flickering oil lamps of old.

The number of train sets suited to halts was also greatly increased. The eight SECR steamcars, which were stored in various places, were pulled out and converted into two articulated pairs for the Sheppey line, and two non-articulated pairs which, after an unsuccessful visit to the Isle of Wight, settled down to thirty years of push-pull service on branch lines in the Gravesend and Sevenoaks area. More ex-LSWR bogie-block sets were broken into push-pull pairs, and various LBSC steam stock rebuilt with control trailers for this work. The Southern seldom wasted anything, and the antiquated set of vestibuled four-wheelers which had been working the Sheppey line was split into two push-pull fitted pairs for use in the Isle of Wight. Soon after arrival they went on to the Merstone–Ventnor West service, which enabled the stations on this line to become unstaffed halts, Godshill and St Lawrence in 1928, Whitwell in 1941.

The opening of the Torrington–Halwill line in 1925 brought in new halts, at Dunsbear and Meeth, with Watergate and Yarde added in 1926; the original ones were nicely built in stone, but the two additions were in rather poor concrete. This line was to be worked by vestibuled LSWR ex-steamcar stock for most of its life. Other new halts included Rowan for a housing estate at the foot of the Dyke branch, Maddaford Moor on Dartmoor, and Sandsfoot Castle on Portland. A halt with full-length platforms was opened at Paulsgrove for a racecourse near Portsmouth, though because of the war it only saw six years' service. There was also a new halt at Stoke Junction, opened with the Allhallows branch which diverged at that point of the Port Victoria line; at Ashley Heath near Ringwood; and for work-people at Waddon Marsh near Croydon Gasworks, Kemsley for the paper mills, Hillsea near Portsmouth. An odd little wooden halt at

Farringdon on the Meon Valley line officially opened in 1931, but it was so uncharacteristic of the SR that it may have been part of the earlier goods station.

Meanwhile experiments were made with new forms of railcar which might be suited to halt work: a four-wheel Drewry car was put on the Lydd lines, but soon sold; a Sentinel bogie steamcar was tried on the Dyke branch, but could not cope and, after a stint on the Westerham branch, was taken out of service. A Michelin 10-wheeled rubber-tyred petrol car had trials in the Alton area but was not purchased. The fact was that the push-pull train, now powered by 'D1' 0–4–2Ts and 'O2', 'M7', 'R'/'R1' and 'D3' 0–4–4Ts, was more reliable and more flexible.

In 1930 came the first electrified halts, Stone Crossing and Swanscombe on the North Kent line and Morden on the West Croydon–Wimbledon. Stone Crossing was left as it was, but at Swanscombe the old wooden halt was abandoned and a large new concrete halt built further down the line. When the main line to Three Bridges was electrified, the old halt at Salfords was given up and a new one built nearby, which later became a station. As the electrification reached the West Coast line in 1938, all the halts were progressively rebuilt in concrete with platforms at least 260 ft long.

In 1928 a new halt was opened at Aylesham on the Dover–Faversham line, for a housing project in the East Kent Coalfield; this was one of the most palatial halts, with large brick waiting rooms and wooden ticket offices on both platforms, and at least one express train to London.

Some de-manning of stations began. One such in 1936 was Latchley, mentioned before as one variously described as a halt and a station; now Latchley, with no parcels service and the siding only taking wagon-loads not requiring handling, was definitely a halt in the RCH Handbook, but it remained a station in the SR timetables. Other stations turned into halts were Hothfield and Brookland; on the other hand, Bingham Road Halt on the Woodside–Selsdon line, after twenty years as a rotting wooden halt with no trains, was rebuilt in concrete as a station.

Train services for halts in SR days were quite good; almost all had the same service as stations on the same line. There were exceptions; on the Hastings–Rye service Snailham, Doleham and Three Oaks halts did badly, with only two trains per day. At the other end of the spectrum, Lucas Terrace Halt near Plymouth still had an LSW-style 'tramcar' service, 27 trains each way (28 on Wednesdays). However, SR timetabling was never simple: Chevening Halt on the Westerham branch had 10 trains which ran every day, six on Saturdays only, five not on Saturdays, and two on Wednesdays only.

When on 1st July, 1930 the SR took over the stations of the former Somerset & Dorset Railway, there were five recently-opened halts included: on the main line, Shoscombe, Stourpaine, Charlton Marshall, Corfe Mullen; and Bawdrip on the Bridgwater branch. Some ex-MR 0–4–4Ts had been fitted for push-and-pull working when these were opened in 1928/9. The SR added another at Creekmoor, and later downgraded Masbury, Spetisbury and Polsham stations to halts.

The Second World War produced some new halts: Idmiston near Porton Down, Longcross (Virginia Water), Woodcroft (Rowlands Castle), and Hamble on Southampton Water. The war also saw the end of Bishopstone Beach Halt, which was in an area handed over to the army; however, although they managed to demolish the station buildings and most of nearby Tide Mills village, the platforms remained. Upper Halliford Halt on the Shepperton branch, opened in 1944, seems to have been the last to be put up by the Southern Railway.

Longfield Halt, opened in 1913, as it was in 1932, with a Gravesend–Swanley train, formed of SECR ex-steamcar stock, but not working push-pull. *Author's Collection*

Mountfield Halt on the Hastings line opened in 1923 and was never rebuilt in concrete before closing in 1969. Tickets were issued from a lean-to on the crossing-keeper's house beyond the level crossing. *Lens of Sutton*

Meeth Halt, one of the original 1925 ND&CJLR halts on the Torrington–Halwill line, was built in stone and – unusually – on a curve. *Lens of Sutton*

Chapter Five

British Rail Days and the End of the 'Halt'

When Nationalisation came in 1948, the new Southern Region acquired a number of halts besides those remaining from the old Companies. One immediate though short-lived addition was the East Kent Light Railway. As mentioned earlier, this was a line on which nobody could agree as to which stops were halts. The only one recognised by all was Poison Cross Halt; but this was in fact a block post and the train staff for the Sandwich Road branch was kept on the platform. It was opened in 1925 and saw only a few trains per week for three years before it closed. Other stopping places mentioned as halts in articles, but not recognised as such by Bradshaw, were Knowlton, Eastry South and Elmton; also Tilmanstone Colliery which was not in the public tables.

On the former Kent & East Sussex Railway, the only stops regarded as halts were Salehurst Platform near Robertsbridge, and Junction Road, a little further towards Bodiam.

Two lines which had previous SR connections also came within the Region: the Didcot, Newbury & Southampton Railway, with halts at Pinewood and Worthy Down; and the Midland & South Western Junction Railway, with halts at Collingbourne Kingston, Chiseldon Camp and Chedworth, on the Andover Junction–Cheltenham line.

Later boundary revisions brought in some halts from the Great Western. Monkton & Came, Upwey Wishing Well and Radipole were on the Dorchester–Weymouth line which had been worked over by SR trains, but they did not stop at the halts. On the Abbotsbury branch there was Coryates Halt, and north of Dorchester on the Westbury line, Thornford Bridge and Chetnole. The Salisbury–Westbury line had a halt at Dilton Marsh near Westbury.

De-manning of stations continued, and in most cases the station became a halt: Greatstone-on-Sea, Lydd-on-Sea, and Brasted on the Westerham line. However, the reverse was not the case; many halts were now busy places with ticket offices, but they did not for the time being become stations. The concept of the Halt was still alive, nevertheless; in 1956 Ampress Works Halt was put up on the Lymington branch (though not in public tables) and in 1958 Hardley Halt on the Totton–Fawley line. The Region also paid attention to keeping push-pull trains going; as the older sets became time-expired, the barrel was dredged for stock to replace them. Various ex-SECR carriages, LSWR straight-sided corridor stock and 'Ironclads' were used. Finally in 1959/61 a series of 20 sets were made up from Maunsell corridor and vestibule stock.

In 1955 the Meon Valley line was closed for passenger traffic, and with it went Farringdon Halt, at 65 ft the shortest public platform still open. Knowle Halt near Fareham had also been served by the Meon Valley trains, but this was not closed. It was an oddity, a single platform facing three running lines, one a reversible line from the Meon Valley through a shaky former main line tunnel, and the two tracks laid in 1907 to by-pass the tunnel. A cross-over had been put in in 1921, so trains to and from Eastleigh could reach the halt; however, the service after 1955 was mean in the extreme: one train each way on Sundays, one Up and two Down on Thursdays, and only one Up each other day. The halt finally closed in 1964.

Between 1948 and 1960 twenty SR branch lines were closed, and many halts went with them. For many survivors there were special reasons; those on the Torrington–Halwill line stayed open because of the clay traffic. By 1960 Meeth Halt had only two trains, though Dunsbear, Yarde and Watergate had four because of the workmen's trains from Torrington. Needless to say, all the halts along the South Coast were alive and well. On the Exmouth service, St James' Park, only half-a-mile out of Exeter, had only six trains, but Polsloe Bridge had 25. One had to look at the former SDJR halts to see the real old-fashioned approach. Masbury Halt near the famed summit of the main line showed no booked trains in Bradshaw, but one train was allowed to pick up 'on timely advice being given' to the signalman; one other could set down if the guard was told. Shoscombe managed to get eight trains, Creekmoor also; but Stourpaine only four plus one 'set down on notice', Spetisbury three and one 'on notice', Corfe Mullen only one and no conditionals. If you lived there, you *had* to take the 8.55 am and come back on the 5.51 pm – but of course there were buses. The newly-opened Hardley Halt on the Fawley line was given only two trains – but they were the only passenger trains along this line, which saw mostly oil traffic.

On the Dover line Snowdown, which had remained a halt, got the same service as Aylesham which had become a station. Only on the West Coast line out of Brighton did the original grand concept remain; halt-stopping trains were different from the semi-fasts. Not that the halts could complain; on the West Worthing service there were halt-stopping trains through the 24 hours, from 12.10 am to 11.40 pm. For most of the day they were half-hourly. At the other end of the line, the Chichester–Portsmouth halts had mostly an hourly service. Hilsea had only morning and evening trains – but what a service! Between 6.59 am and 8.55 am, with trains coming in from Fareham as well as Chichester, there were 14 trains from Hilsea Halt to Portsmouth, with some headways down to three minutes. On the

Sheerness branch, Swale Halt had a train every hour, Kemsley Halt twice as many. In the Ascot area, Longcross and Winnersh got the same trains as the stations, though they were not served after about eight in the evening, while the stations remained open until midnight. On the West Croydon–Wimbledon line, Morden Road and Waddon Marsh halts had half-hourly trains – though Morden Road had none on Saturdays.

The only line with a cavalier attitude to halts was Rye–Hastings, where almost all trains missed out one of the three halts. The result was that one could not travel from Winchelsea Halt to Doleham Halt until 10.15am, and on Saturdays no train stopped at both Doleham Halt and Three Oaks Halt between 3pm and 10.30pm, though during that time five trains stopped at one or other. Local residents complained strongly and shortly after, all 16 trains were stopping everywhere.

In 1961 closings included Stoke Junction Halt. This had been built at the junction with the Allhallows line off the Port Victoria branch, and latterly most trains had run to and from Allhallows via Port Victoria, reversing at Stoke Junction. When the new station was opened in 1951 at Grain refinery, the workmen's evening train did the same, so that one had the odd situation in which the same train called at Stoke Junction Halt at 4.44pm, 4.59pm and 5.04pm!

One late BR halt, which was on a former SR line but now in Western Region, was somewhat bizarre. A very short rail-level 'halt' was established in 1964 at Boscarne Junction, where the former SR and GWR lines from their Bodmin stations joined *en route* for Wadebridge. A 4-wheeled AC railbus was put on to there from Bodmin North; passengers walked a short distance to another halt put up on the former GWR side of the junction, to join a DMU service from Bodmin Road to Padstow. However, this all came to an end on 30th January, 1967.

Following the transfer in 1963 of the SR lines west and south of Exeter to the Western Region, in 1965 a number of stations were unstaffed and appeared as halts in the WR timetables: on the Exeter–Plymouth line via Lydford, Sampford Courtenay Halt, Bridestowe Halt, St Budeaux Halt; on the Ilfracombe line, Morchard Road Halt and Chapelton Halt; on the Wadebridge line, Otterham Halt.

A surprising addition to the list was Bodmin North Halt, but then the GWR had never worried about dubbing terminus stations 'halts'. This former LSWR station was a halt for only a year, before being closed. It seems that in the winter period 1965/6 the Boscarne Exchange Platform was not in use, as the tables showed the only two trains serving Dunsbear Halt and Bodmin North Halt as coming from

Stone Crossing Halt on the Dartford–Gravesend Central line, in 1930. The incomplete upper-quadrant signals are for the impending electrification; note that the old lower-quadrant signal, left of the lamp, was in the middle of the platform. *Author's Collection*

Brookland Halt about 1950, after the former station buildings and signal cabin had been removed; original down platform in foreground. *Lens of Sutton*

Bodmin Road and doing a quick trip up the other line after reversal at Boscarne Junction. However, the platform was back in use in June, with a better service to Bodmin North.

In 1965 the stations on the Exmouth branch, except Topsham, were under-manned and were shown as halts in the WR timetable: Exton Halt and Lympstone Halt. At the same time the conductor-guards were issued with Omniprinter ticket machines, probably the first on any ex-SR line. The track was also singled (Exmouth Junction–Topsham, 1972, Topsham–Exmouth, 1968), and after a few years as an all-halt line, it became finally an all-station line when the suffix 'Halt' was dropped in the early seventies. Newton Poppleford on the line to Exmouth via Tipton St John also became a halt.

Dilton Marsh Halt near Westbury, which, as stated above, came into the Southern Region with the boundary revisions, was an odd one. The platforms were very much staggered, with a 200-yard walk between them; and even in BR days there was a printed notice outside stating that tickets were to be obtained from Mrs Roberts at a private house seven houses up the hill. When it was transferred to the SR it was still wooden, but at some time after 1970 it was rebuilt with steel decking and ramps.

The concept of the Halt began to wither away in the late 'sixties; articles and announcements often did not differentiate. Whereas when, in 1955, Brasted had become a halt, new name-boards for 'Brasted Halt' were supplied, now stations becoming unmanned simply went into limbo. Some were stripped of their old buildings and reduced to bare platforms with pre-formed glass shelters – but they did not become 'halts'. By the 'seventies the word was no longer to be found in the timetables. This was a national policy; when Clinker produced his 'Register of Closed Stations' in 1978, he recorded that there were only five official halts left, all in Scotland. When in March 1976 a 'halt' called Lympstone Commando was created on the Exmouth line (not officially a public one) it was referred to as a 'platform', thus coming full circle to the days before 1903.

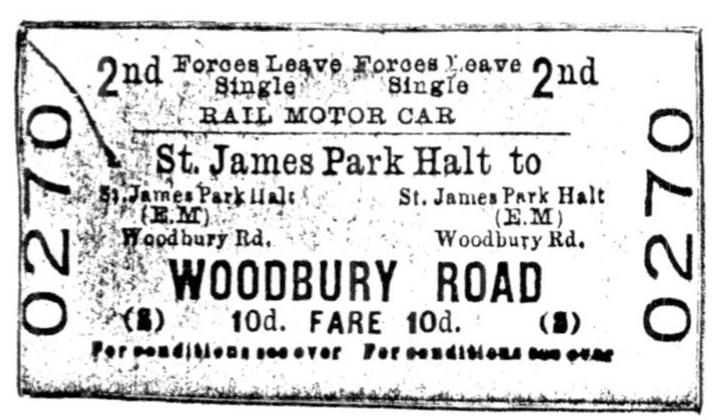

Farringdon Halt on the Meon Valley line about 1955; it was officially opened in 1931 but was probably in use for workpeople earlier; note goods station behind. *Lens of Sutton*

Idmiston Halt, a war-time (1943) halt for Porton Down workers; previously they had travelled over a narrow gauge railway from Porton station. *Lens of Sutton*

Chapter Six

Conclusion

The pure theory of halt-cum-railmotor was put into practice only briefly; this was by the LSWR, whose steamcars could not take tail-loads, and who had at least some branches with close halts and frequent cars. Once the Companies had opted for stock that could take tail traffic (and that included the SECR steamcars), platforms had to be longer, and turn-rounds extended for possible shunting movements. Thereafter halts became less of a philosophy, more of a cheap station. This was probably inevitable, for the original conception depended on the assumption that one way or another passenger traffic would remain on rails; once most of it had transferred to buses and cars, that idea was dead. By the time much of the push-and-pull stock could be found working as conventional trains, and halts were being extended to take eight coaches, there was not much left of the basic idea. However, enough did persist to enable many branches to stay open longer than they would otherwise have done and, like the telephone box at a lonely moorland crossroads, some performed a service for the few people who used them that was worth a lot more than the few pence the guard took in.

Chevening Halt in 1930, before rebuilding in concrete; the train is hauled by an '01' 0–6–0 at a time when the branch was not motor-worked. *Author's Collection*

Swale Halt: *above*, in its original form opened as Kings Ferry Bridge Halt in 1922, and *below*, the new halt in 1960; note new bridge, and road moved from east to west side.

Lens of Sutton

Chapter Seven

Construction of Halts

The early halts were all of timber; cheapness was the watchword and the SECR used mainly old sleepers. If on a double line, there were separate entrances to each platform to avoid a footbridge. After a few years, small shelters were added. Lighting was by oil, though later some were converted to gas or electricity depending on availability, and in a few cases Tilley pressure lamps were used. If a halt could not be lit, trains called only in daylight. In many cases the guard of the last train extinguished lamps as the train proceeded.

The above was standard for halts built for a railmotor programme; however, a few single ones were put up for special reasons unconnected to railmotors, and all kinds of constructions were used: earth fill behind sleeper fronts, brick, stone, corrugated iron and, of course later, concrete.

Some halts issued tickets and there would be a small booth, or two if it was double line. In general, the Companies had a good idea of the sort of people who would use a halt, and thus they varied from bare platforms for workmen or the odd hiker, to long platforms with several seats and one or two shelters for well-used halts.

Halts were originally intended for one railcar only, so were only about 70ft long, but over the years all were extended and any low ones raised. These changes can be noted in photographs, though of course not all halts were lucky in that respect. Hurst Green Halt, for example, was photographed a dozen times in its existence, Seven Stones not at all until after it closed.

The Southern Railway, with its passion for pre-cast concrete, devised a standard halt construction, with pre-cast 'legs', paving slabs, back walls, shelters etc., all slotted in like children's bricks, the only variation being length. However, a number of halts, especially the larger ones, were rebuilt in a different style, with concrete platform fronts and fill behind. In fact, variations in origin, site, purpose and history meant that remarkably few halts were exactly the same in appearance.

Doleham Halt about 1970, showing down platform rebuilt in concrete, and the up platform still timber; the up line was later taken out. *Lens of Sutton*

Morden was a station on the West Croydon–Wimbledon line, made a halt in 1919, renamed Morden Road later, then stripped of its buildings in the seventies. With its tiny shelter it is once again a 'station'. *Lens of Sutton*

Chapter Eight

Tickets to and from Halts

Old railway tickets have proved a useful source of information, as some have revealed that stops shown in the tables as stations had become halts even though the nameboards may not have been changed.

All three Companies issued thin Bell Punch type tickets for their early railmotor-cum-halt services, some of which were still of this type in SR days, and a few under BR. However, as time went on, guard-issued tickets for halts were increasingly of the Edmondson card type, even though many of these retained the vertical format of the Bell Punch tickets. Tickets in the collection of Mr J. Britton show that there were three types of Bell Punch in use: those quoting only one journey, e.g. LBSC 'Brighton & Dyke Junction 2*d*'; alternative journeys, e.g. 'Beeches Halt to West Croydon or Banstead and Return', with a large figure 6*d* over the face; also ones such as used on the West Croydon-Wimbledon line which gave all stations or halts between which the nominated fare was valid. On the Woodside & South Croydon line the tickets printed all stops with the fare against them, 1*d*, 1½*d* or 2*d* from the point of issue.

The SR tickets for the Melcombe Regis–Easton service were copied from an early GWR design and had the fare at the top, and on the right a list of stations and halts; the correct one to which the fare applied had to be punched. Oddly, one was headed 'Southern & GW Rlys (E&CH)' although few people can have heard of the Easton & Church Hope Railway.

Bell Punch tickets have been noted for the following services: Plymouth area, Bournemouth area, Exeter area, Callington branch, West Croydon–Wimbledon, Hastings–Rye, Kemp Town, Seaford branch, Sheppey Light, Lee-on-Solent, Easton branch, Exmouth-branch, Portsmouth–Chichester, Horsham–Three Bridges, Tunbridge Wells area, Dyke branch, Eastbourne–St Leonards, Tooting Loops, Brighton–Worthing, Ventnor West–Newport IOW.

That differing tickets were issued at various times is shown by the existence of a Bell Punch ticket for Lions Holt Halt to Whipton Bridge Halt, and an Edmondson's card for Lions Holt Halt to Exmouth (headed 'LSWR Railmotor No. 1'). An interesting Edmondson's LBSC ticket is headed 'Motor Car Service Tunbridge Wells' though it is for Roffey Road Halt & Littlehaven Halt or Littlehaven Halt & Horsham.

In BR days, Edmondson's cards in vertical format and still headed 'Rail Motor Car' were in use on the Sheppey Light and Ventnor West branch. An interesting one is a BR return issued for Denton Halt to Uralite Halt which is headed 'Early Morning Return (Shift)'.

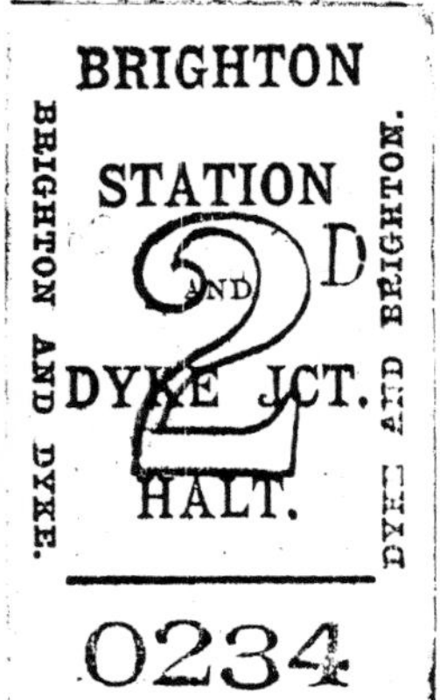

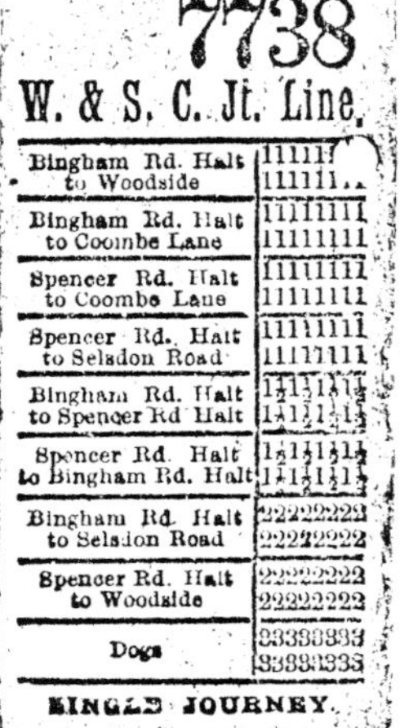

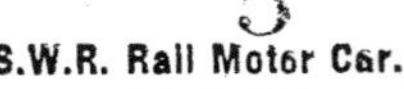

This Ticket is issued subject to the Regulations and Conditions stated in the Company's Time Tables & Bills. (S. 1

First Class Single
FARE 3d. Between
LIONS HOLT HALT
&
WHIPTON BRIDGE
HALT

This Ticket must be punched in the Section to which the Passenger is entitled to travel and must be shown on demand.

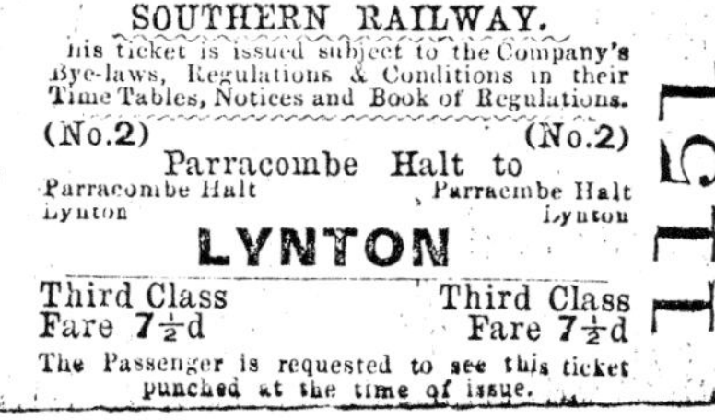

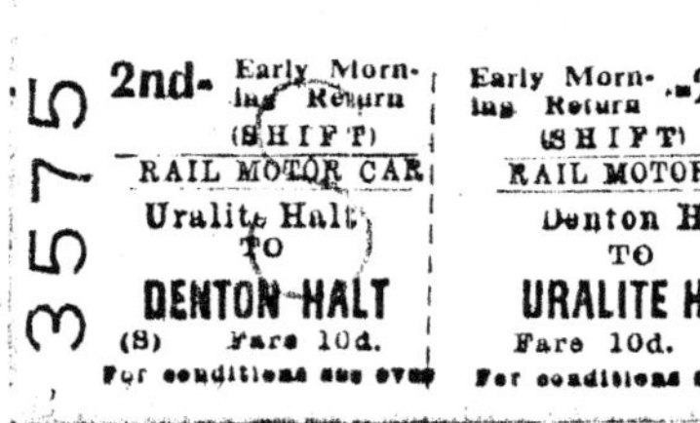

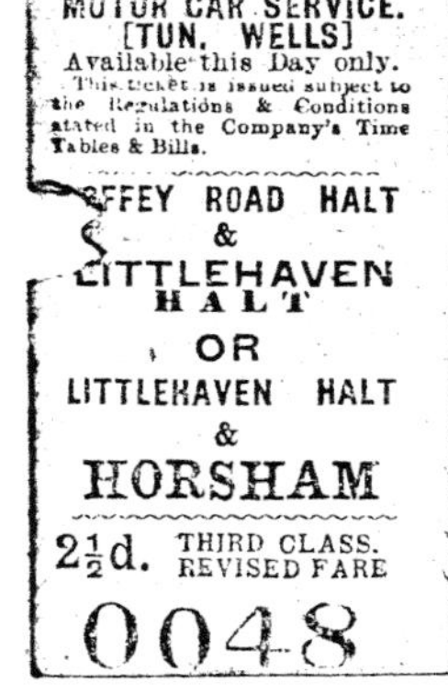

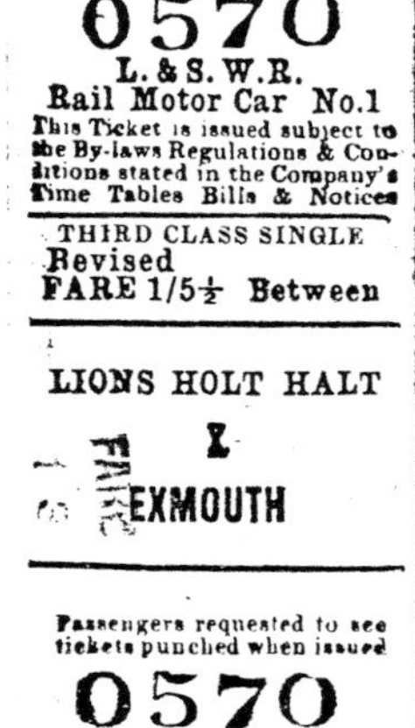

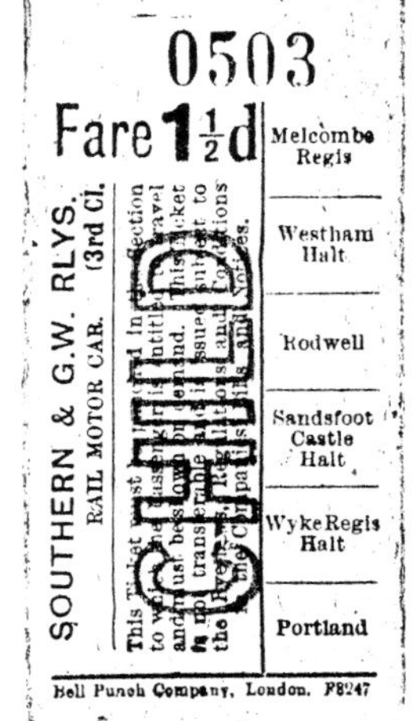

Chapter Nine

Non-Public Platforms

There were always a number of 'platforms' on the SR which were neither proper stations nor halts, being either open only on occasions or available only to certain people. Stations for race traffic were an obvious example, such as Gatwick Racecourse and Kempton Park, or extra and separate platforms attached to stations, such as Westenhanger, Ascot West, Plumpton and Esher. There were also platforms for military use, such as Deepcut and Blackdown on a short-lived extension from Bisley, built by the War Department – these two were in fact for a few months from 8th August, 1918 LSWR property. Then there was a platform at the end of a short branch from Slades Green known variously as Trench Warfare Filling Station or Crayford Ness, which, though worked to by the SECR was never their property. There were several stations and halts on the Longmoor Military Railway between Bordon and Liss, and one at Manston RAF airfield which actually had through trains to London.

Hospitals and golf courses also had their platforms, most of which were public enough to be in the present work. The longest-lived privately-owned platforms were on the branch from Brookwood to the London Necropolis (one for Catholics, one for C of E) which were open from 1858 until 1941, when the corresponding private platform at Waterloo, and the train itself, was bombed.

Most of these fall outside the scope of the present work, but it is interesting to note that beyond or below the level of official halts, there were other places where trains stopped; one has even heard of a place where trains habitually halted to allow people to indulge in illegal cock-fighting at a remote spot.

Treloar's Hospital Platform. *Lens of Sutton*

Lydd-on-Sea Halt. *Lens of Sutton*

Littlehaven Halt. *Lens of Sutton*

Chapter Ten

Gazetteer of Halts

This shows the position and opening and closing dates, also any unusual feature of construction or traffic. Where the exact location may have been forgotten, extra details are given.

Closing dates given are those for the first day of no service, unless there was no Sunday service.

The list covers all halts built by the Southern Railway or its constituent companies, halts opened by BR Southern Region, and Southern Railway stations which became halts in Southern Region. It does not cover GWR halts which came into the Southern Region due to boundary changes, or SR stations which became WR halts. However, a couple of West Country openings by Western Region on former Southern Region lines have been included for interest.

Unless otherwise stated, all halts were originally wooden, except those built after about 1930 which were concrete; any halt surviving to 1930 can be assumed to have been rebuilt in concrete, unless otherwise stated.

The following abbreviations are used: SC–signal cabin; SB–station building; LC–level crossing; FB–footbridge.

Stonehall and Lydden Halt. *Lens of Sutton*

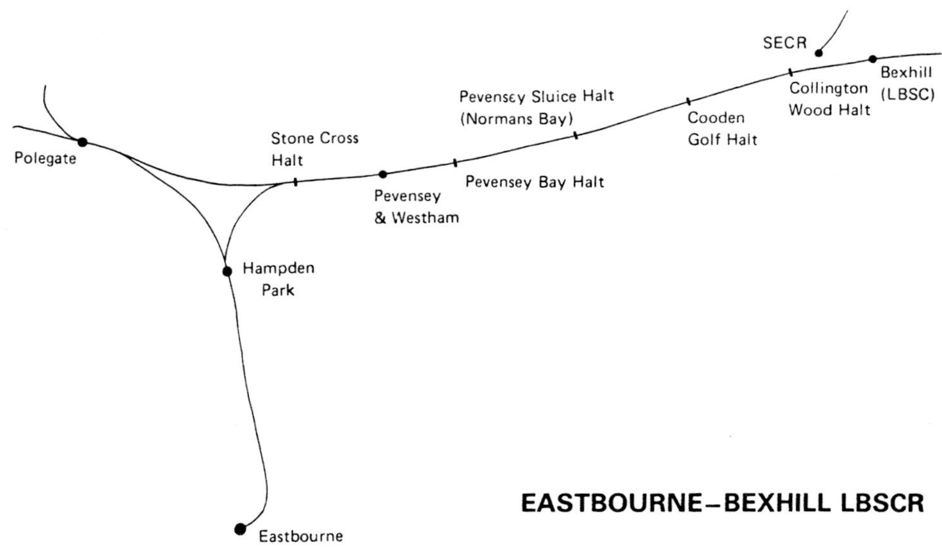
SECR
Bexhill
(LBSC)
Collington
Wood Halt
Pevensey Sluice Halt
(Normans Bay)
Cooden
Golf Halt
Stone Cross
Halt
Polegate
Pevensey Bay Halt
Pevensey
& Westham
Hampden
Park
EASTBOURNE–BEXHILL LBSCR
Eastbourne

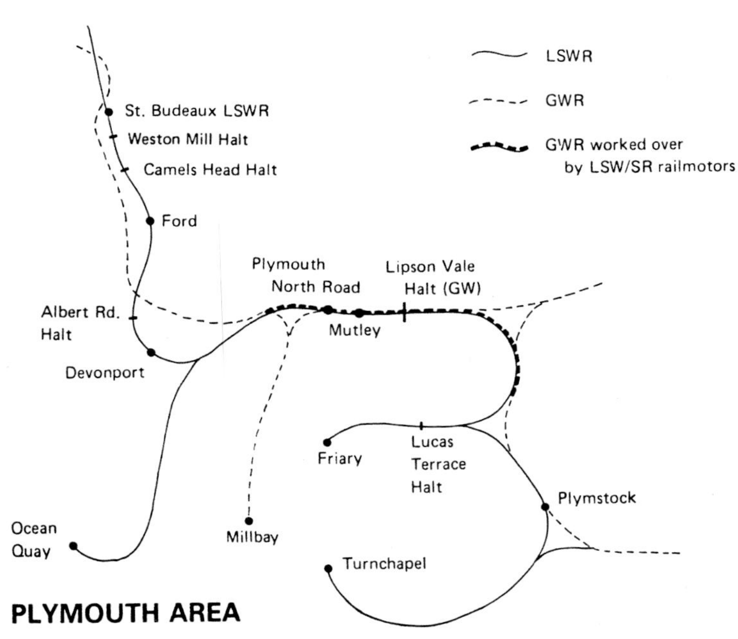
LSWR
GWR
GWR worked over
by LSW/SR railmotors
St. Budeaux LSWR
Weston Mill Halt
Camels Head Halt
Ford
Plymouth
North Road
Lipson Vale
Halt (GW)
Albert Rd.
Halt
Mutley
Devonport
Lucas
Terrace
Halt
Friary
Plymstock
Ocean
Quay
Millbay
Turnchapel
PLYMOUTH AREA

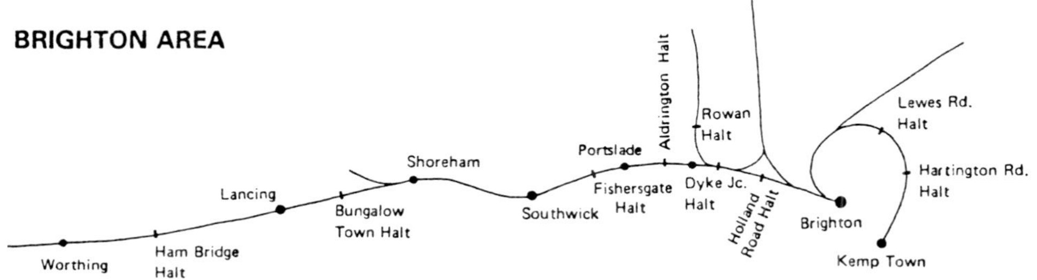
BRIGHTON AREA
Worthing
Ham Bridge Halt
Lancing
Bungalow Town Halt
Shoreham
Southwick
Portslade
Fishersgate Halt
Aldrington Halt
Rowan Halt
Dyke Jc. Halt
Holland Road Halt
Brighton
Lewes Rd. Halt
Hartington Rd. Halt
Kemp Town

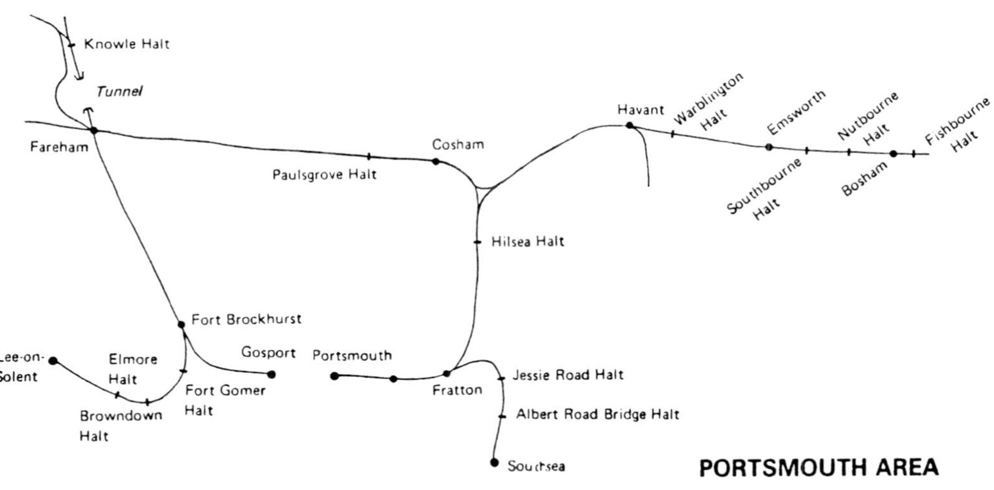
Knowle Halt
Tunnel
Fareham
Paulsgrove Halt
Cosham
Havant
Warblington Halt
Emsworth
Southbourne Halt
Nutbourne Halt
Bosham
Fishbourne Halt
Hilsea Halt
Fort Brockhurst
Lee-on-Solent
Elmore Halt
Browndown Halt
Fort Gomer Halt
Gosport
Portsmouth
Fratton
Jessie Road Halt
Albert Road Bridge Halt
Southsea
PORTSMOUTH AREA

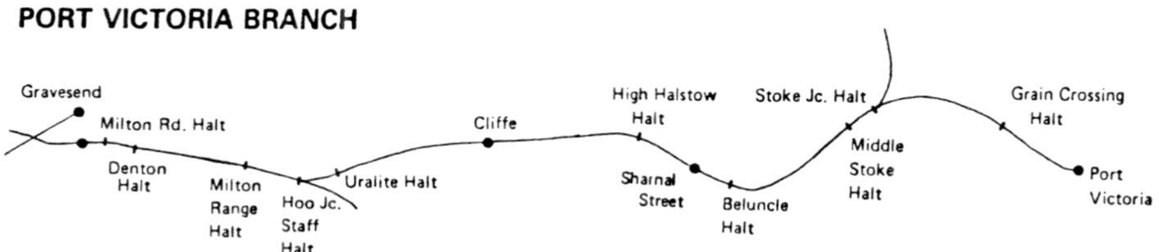
PORT VICTORIA BRANCH
Gravesend
Milton Rd. Halt
Denton Halt
Milton Range Halt
Hoo Jc. Staff Halt
Uralite Halt
Cliffe
High Halstow Halt
Sharnal Street
Beluncle Halt
Stoke Jc. Halt
Middle Stoke Halt
Grain Crossing Halt
Port Victoria

SNAPPER HALT. L & B. RLY.

Snapper Halt in its original form. *Lens of Sutton*

Middle Stoke Halt. *Lens of Sutton*

A

ALBERT ROAD HALT (1st October, 1906–13th January, 1947). Between Devonport and Ford on the Devonport–St Budeaux line, ½m from Devonport.

ALBERT ROAD BRIDGE HALT (1st July, 1904–8th August, 1914). Between Jessie Road Halt and East Southsea on the branch from Fratton, ¾m from Fratton. Platform on down line only (up line out of use).

ALDRINGTON HALT (3rd September, 1905). Opened as Dyke Junction Halt, renamed 1932. Between Hove and Portslade, ½m from Hove.

AMPRESS WORKS HALT (1st October, 1956). On Lymington branch, 1m from Lymington Town, for workers at Wellworthy factory; not in public tables; concrete, chain-link fencing.

ASH GREEN HALT (8th October, 1849–4th July, 1937). Former station, became halt 1926; between Ash Junction and Tongham on Guildford–Farnham line.

ASHLEY HEATH HALT (1st April, 1927–3rd May, 1964). Between Ringwood and West Moors on old Brockenhurst–Bournemouth line, 1½m from Ringwood. Goods depot.

ATLANTIC PARK HOSTEL HALT (30th October, 1929–?). Single down platform on site of present Southampton Airport station, Eastleigh, for immigrants to USA from nearby camp. Not public.

AYLESHAM HALT (1st July, 1928). Between Snowdown Halt and Adisham on Faversham–Dover line, 1m from Adisham. For colliery housing estate. Large brick shelters, wooden booking offices, both platforms. Rebuilt as station *c.*1960.

B

BANDON HALT (11th June, 1906–7th June, 1914). Between Wallington and Waddon on the Wimbledon–Sutton line, 1m W. of Waddon. Bandon SC nearby.

BAWDRIP HALT (October 1923–1st December, 1952). Between Bridgwater and Cossington on the SDJR branch. Always concrete, solid platform.

BEDDINGTON LANE HALT (22nd October, 1855). 'Beddington Station' to 1887, 'Beddington Lane Station' to 1919, then halt. Between Mitcham Junction and Waddon Marsh Halt on the West Croydon-

–Sutton line, 1¼m from Waddon Marsh. Had SC; train staff station, but no loop. Goods line on N side from LC to West Croydon.

BEDHAMPTON HALT (1st April, 1906). Between Havant and Hilsea Halt, ¾m W of Havant.

BEECHES HALT: see Carshalton Beeches.

BELTRING & BRANBRIDGES HALT (1st September, 1909). Between Paddock Wood and Yalding on Maidstone line, 1½m from Yalding. Remains wooden. Ticket office at LC.

BELUNCLE HALT (July 1906–4th December, 1961). Between Sharnal Street and Middle Stoke Halt on Port Victoria line. Adjacent to existing Miskin Sidings. Small ticket office and old van body as store.

BINGHAM ROAD HALT (1st September, 1906–15th March, 1915). Between Woodside and Coombe Lane on Selsdon Road line. Re-opened as station 30th September, 1935; closed 1983.

BISHOPSTONE BEACH HALT (1st June, 1864–1st January, 1942). 'Bishopstone Station' to 1st August, 1922, then 'Bishopstone Halt', closed 26th September, 1938; re-opened as Bishopstone Beach Halt April 1939, summers only. Full length brick rendered platforms, latterly shelters on each; extra face (disused) to up bay. Situated at LC of track to Tide Mills, to which a branch once ran from the sidings.

BLEAN & TYLER HILL HALT (1908–1st January, 1931). Between South Street Halt and Canterbury West on Whitstable Harbour line, ½m N of the tunnel.

BOSCARNE EXCHANGE PLATFORMS (May, 1964–30th January, 1967). Comprised a rail-level 'platform' on the ex-SR side of Dunmere Junction and a normal level halt on the ex-GWR side; DMUs to and from Padstow–Bodmin Road stopped for passengers to exchange to cars to and from Boscarne–Bodmin North Halt. Not used in winter. Became Western Region territory in 1963.

BRAMBLEDOWN HALT (March, 1905–4th December, 1950). Between Eastchurch and Minster-on-Sea on Sheppey branch, 1m E of latter. Siding. Always wooden.

BRAMSHOT HALT (10th May, 1913 for golfers, public 3rd July, 1938, closed 6th October, 1946). Adjacent to golf course, also later a military camp. Located alongside main road ½m E of Fleet Pond, between Fleet and Farnborough stations.

BRASTED HALT (7th July, 1881–30th October, 1961). Former station between Chevening Halt and Westerham, made a halt in 1955.

BROOKLAND HALT (7th December, 1881–6th March, 1967). Former station between Appledore and Lydd Town, 2½m from Appledore;

became a halt c.1930. Passing loop, SB on down side, shelter up side, SC up end. Loop removed and down platform disused c.1950.

BROWNDOWN HALT (12th May, 1894–1st May, 1930). Between Elmore Halt and Fort Gomer Halt on Lee-on-Solent branch. Located S of Alverstoke Road just W of LC.

BUNGALOW TOWN HALT (1st October, 1910–15th July, 1940). Between Shoreham and Lancing, 1 m W of Shoreham. Closed 1st January, 1933; re-opened as Shoreham Airport Halt 1st July, 1935.

C

CAFFYNS HALT (December, 1906–30th September, 1935). Between Woody Bay and Lynton, 1½m N of Woody Bay, to serve golf course; public from 1916. Located on the road from A39 to W. Ilkerton. On a 1 in 50 gradient; trains preferred not to stop.

CAMELS HEAD HALT (1st November, 1906–4th May, 1942). Between Ford and St Budeaux on Devonport line, ¾m from St Budeaux.

CARISBROOKE HALT (20th July, 1889–21st September, 1953). Former station between Newport IOW and Calbourne on Freshwater line. Called a halt in articles but not so in time-tables.

CARSHALTON BEECHES HALT (1st October, 1906). Between Wallington and Sutton, opened as Beeches Halt, changed to Carshalton Beeches Station on opening of overhead electric 1st April, 1925.

CEMENT MILLS HALT (c.1909–21st February, 1966). On the Cowes Line, IOW, between Newport and Mill Hill, for workers at Medina Cement Mills. Very short wooden platform at junction with mill siding. Not in public tables but could be used by public on request.

CHARLTON MARSHALL HALT (9th July, 1928–17th September, 1956). Between Blandford and Spetisbury on SDJ line, 1¾m S of Blandford.

CHERITON HALT (1st May, 1908–1st December, 1915; 14th June, 1920–1st February, 1941; 7th October, 1946–16th June, 1947). Between Lyminge and Shorncliffe on Elham Valley line, ½m from Shorncliffe, almost at junction.

CHESTFIELD & SWALECLIFFE HALT (6th July, 1930). Between Whitstable and Herne Bay on former LCD main line, 2¼m from Herne Bay.

CHEVENING HALT (16th April, 1906–30th October, 1961). Between Dunton Green and Brasted on the Westerham branch, located ½m SW of Chevening Crossroads.

Dunmere Halt. *Lens of Sutton*

Polsloe Bridge Halt. *Lens of Sutton*

CHILSWORTHY HALT (1st June, 1909–5th December, 1966). Between Gunnislake and Latchley on Calstock branch, 1 m from Gunnislake. Called a halt in most references, including SR Bell Punch tickets, but not in Bradshaw.

CHISLET COLLIERY HALT (1920–4th October, 1971). Between Sturry and Grove Ferry on Canterbury–Minster line, 2 m from Sturry. Colliery closed 1969, halt renamed Chislet Halt.

CHURCH MANORWAY HALT (1st January, 1917–31st December, 1919). Between Abbey Wood and Plumstead on N. Kent Line; for munitions workers. Two crossovers; some trains from London reversed there.

CLYST ST MARY & DIGBY HALT (1st June, 1908–27th September, 1948). Between Polsloe Bridge Halt and Topsham on Exmouth line, at N side of bridge over A35, mainly for Digby Mental Hospital.

COLLINGTON HALT (11th September, 1905–1st September, 1906; 1st June, 1911–(still open)). Opened as Collington Wood Halt; reopened 1911 as West Bexhill Halt, reverted 1929 to Collington Halt. Between Cooden Beach and Bexhill Central, ¾ m from latter.

COODEN HALT (11th September, 1905). Opened as Cooden Golf Halt, later Cooden Halt and finally 7th July, 1935 Cooden Beach Station. Between Normans Bay and Collington Halts, 2¼ m E of Bexhill Central.

CORFE MULLEN HALT (5th July, 1928–17th September, 1956). Between Bailey Gate and Broadstone on SDJ line, 3 m S of Bailey Gate.

CREEKMOOR HALT (19th June, 1933–17th March, 1966). Between Broadstone and Poole on SDJ line, 1¼ m S of Broadstone; for nearby factory.

CROW PARK HALT (1918–1920). Between Bursledon and Swanwick on Portsmouth–Southampton line. Served a factory at river end of cutting N of Swanwick.

D

DENTON HALT (July 1906–4th December, 1961). Between Milton Road and Milton Range, 1¼ m from Gravesend. Called Denton Road 1914–19.

DENVILLE HALT (see Warblington)

DOLEHAM HALT (1st July, 1907). Opened as Guestling Halt, between Three Oaks and Snailham Halts on the Hastings–Rye line, 4¾ m from Hastings. Westbound platform rebuilt in concrete, eastbound not. Singled 1979.

DUNMERE HALT (2nd July, 1906–30th January, 1967). Between Bodmin North and Nanstallon Halt, 1½m from Bodmin. GWR 'pagoda' shelter.

DUNSBEAR HALT (27th July, 1925–1st March, 1965). Between Yarde Halt and Petrockstowe on Torrington-Halwill line; just S of junction with branch to Marland clay works, 2¼m from Petrockstowe. Stone built.

DURLEY HALT (23rd December, 1909–2nd January, 1933). Between Botley and Bishops Waltham, 1½m from Botley.

DYKE JUNCTION HALT: see Aldrington.

E

EAST MALLING HALT (1913). Between West Malling and Barming on the Maidstone line, 1 m E of W. Malling. Not rebuilt in concrete until 1959.

EAST WORTHING HALT: see Ham Bridge.

EBBSFLEET & CLIFFSEND HALT (May, 1908–1st April, 1933). Between Minster Junction and Ramsgate, 1¾m from Minster Junction station.

ELMORE HALT (11th April, 1910–1st May, 1930). Between Browndown Halt and Lee-on-Solent, ¾m from Lee. Situated at point where railway joined coast road. Rendered brick platform.

F

FARRINGDON HALT (1st May, 1931–7th February, 1955). Between Butts Junction and Tisted on Meon Valley line, 2¾m S of Butts Junction. Farington [*sic*] Platform in Clinker, Farringdon Halt in RCH, Faringdon in some sources. Probably renamed Faringdon to Farringdon 1934. Very short (65 ft) wood platform adjoining existing goods station. Removed on closing for passengers and site used for large concrete goods platform.

FISHBOURNE HALT (1st April, 1906). Between Chichester and Bosham, 1½m W of former.

FISHERSGATE HALT (3rd September, 1905). Between Southwick and Portslade, ½m W of Portslade. Spelt Fishergate on some maps.

FORT GOMER HALT (12th April, 1894–1st May, 1930). Between Fort Brockhurst and Browndown on Lee-on-Solent branch. Originally (to 1909) named Privett. Located at Privett LC.

G

GLYNE GAP HALT (11th September, 1905–1st October, 1915). On the coast line 1¼m E of Bexhill.

GODSHILL HALT (20th July, 1897–15th September, 1952). Former station on Ventnor West branch, between Whitwell and Merstone IOW; made a halt in 1928.

GRAIN CROSSING HALT (1st July, 1906–3rd September, 1951). Between Middle Stoke Halt and Port Victoria, 1½m from latter. LC and ground-frame. (New 1951 Grain Station was 300yds west.) Word 'Crossing' omitted on nameboard.

GREATSTONE-ON-SEA HALT (4th July, 1937–6th March, 1967). Former station, between New Romney and Lydd-on-Sea on 1937 re-routed New Romney branch; made a halt in 1954.

GROGLEY HALT (2nd July, 1906–30th January, 1967). Between Wadebridge and Nanstallon Halt on Bodmin line, 3m from Wadebridge. GWR 'pagoda' shelter. Had ground-frame for junction with Ruthernbridge branch which diverged here.

H

HAMBLE HALT (18th January, 1942). Between Bursledon and Netley on Portsmouth–Southampton line, ¾m from Netley. For aircraft and oil workers.

HAM BRIDGE HALT (3rd September, 1905). Between Worthing and Lancing, 1½m from former. Re-named East Worthing Halt 1949.

HARDLEY HALT (3rd March, 1958–5th April, 1965). Between Hythe (Hants) and Fawley, for oil industry workers.

HARTINGTON ROAD HALT (1st June, 1906–1st June, 1911). Between Lewes Road and Kemp Town. Served a cemetery. Situated 20ch S of Lewes Road.

HARTY ROAD HALT (March, 1905–4th December, 1950). Between Leysdown and Eastchurch on Sheppey line, 1½m E of Eastchurch. LC but no keeper; guard opened gates.

HIGH HALSTOW HALT (July, 1906–4th December, 1961). Between Cliffe and Sharnal Street on Port Victoria line, 1¾m from Cliffe. At existing Wybourne Siding; SC and LC.

HIGH ROCKS HALT (1st June, 1907–5th May, 1952). Between Tunbridge Wells West and Groombridge, 1m from latter. Staggered platforms. Closed 1939–42.

Kemsley Halt. *Lens of Sutton*

Grain Halt, as rebuilt in concrete. *Lens of Sutton*

HILSEA HALT (October, 1937). Between Portcreek Junction and Fratton, 2¼m from latter. For workers only until November, 1941. 'Hilsea Siding' adjacent.

HOLLAND ROAD HALT (3rd September, 1905–7th May, 1956). Between Brighton and Hove, ½m from latter, between Holland Road goods station and Hove loop junction.

HOO JUNCTION STAFF HALT (1956). Between Milton Range and Higham on N. Kent line, in middle of Hoo Junction marshalling yard; staggered platforms.

HOSPITAL HALT (*c.*1920–1965). On Portland–Easton line, near Portland Castle.

HOTHFIELD HALT (1st July, 1884–2nd November, 1959). Former station between Ashford and Charing, 2¾m from latter; made a halt in 1937.

HURST GREEN HALT (1st June, 1907). S of Oxted at junction between East Grinstead and Tunbridge Wells West lines. S of road bridge; closed 12th June, 1961 and station opened N of road bridge.

I

IDMISTON HALT (3rd January, 1943–9th September, 1968). Between Grateley and Porton on LSW main line, ¾m from Porton. Opened to replace MOD railway to complex from Porton station.

IFIELD HALT (1st June, 1907). Opened as Lyons Crossing Halt, closed 1917–20. Between Crawley and Faygate, 1m from Crawley. Became station 1930.

INGRESS ABBEY PLATFORM (*c.*1915–19). On short branch from E of Greenhithe (previously used by Globe Cement Co. and later by a paper works), serving a military hospital.

J

JESSIE ROAD BRIDGE HALT (1st July, 1904–8th August, 1914). Between Fratton and Albert Road Bridge Halt on E. Southsea branch, ¼m from Fratton. Platform on down line only; up line out of use.

K

KEMSLEY HALT (1st January, 1927). Between Sittingbourne and Swale Halt on Sheerness branch, 2m from Sittingbourne. For workers at paper mill. Loop platform, SC, and footbridge added in stages.

Chilsworthy Halt. *Lens of Sutton*

Bedhampton Halt. *Lens of Sutton*

KINGS FERRY BRIDGE HALTS: see Swale Halt

KINGSLEY HALT (7th March, 1906–16th September, 1957). Between Bentley and Bordon, 2m from latter. Sleeper front, filled behind.

KNOWLE HALT (1st May, 1907–6th April, 1964). Between Botley and Fareham, just S of junction with Meon Valley line, 2m from Fareham. Opened as Knowle Asylum Halt, later Knowle Platform to 1942. Single platform facing three lines, Meon Valley line through tunnel and main lines by-passing tunnel. Mainly served by Meon Valley trains, but at various times and after 1955 main line trains called.

L

LAKE HALT (IOW) (*c*.1904). Between Sandown and Shanklin, for cricket matches.

LAKE HALT (September, 1918–*c*.1920). Between Hamworthy and Hamworthy Junction, 1m S of latter, for shipyard workers, on line closed to passengers in 1896.

LATCHLEY HALT (2nd March, 1908–7th November, 1966). Between Gunnislake and Stoke Climsland on Callington branch (PDSWJR), 2m from Gunnislake. Formerly Cox's Park Depot, East Cornwall Railway. A station in some sources.

LEWES ROAD HALT (1st September, 1873–2nd January, 1933). Former station on Kemp Town branch, just S of junction. Probably a halt from 1905. Closed 1917–19. Had a platform with SB serving down trains, island platform between tracks serving only up.

LIONS HOLT HALT (1906). Between Exeter and Pinhoe, just W of Black Boy tunnel, ½m from Exeter Queen Street. Became St James' Park Halt 1946. Brick shelters.

LIPSON VALE HALT: a GWR halt between Lipson Junction and Plymouth Mutley, called at by LSWR trains and tickets to it issued on LSW railmotors. Listed equivocally in RCH (1938) as 'Lipson Vale Halt (GW), Company SR'.

LITTLEHAVEN HALT (1st June, 1907). Between Horsham and Faygate, 1m from former. Opened as Rusper Road Crossing Halt, Littlehaven Crossing Halt 7/1907, then Littlehaven 12/1907. Not concrete until 1963.

LONGCROSS HALT (*c*.1940). Between Sunningdale and Virginia Water, for Army; public 21st September, 1942.

LONGFIELD HALT (1st June, 1913–3rd August, 1953). Between Southfleet and Fawkham Junction on Gravesend West Street branch, ¾m from junction. Located under bridge on Longfield–Betsham road.

Snailham Halt. *Lens of Sutton*

Brambledown Halt. *Lens of Sutton*

LUCAS TERRACE HALT (October, 1905–10th September, 1951). On Turnchapel branch, ¾m from Plymouth Friary, just W of junction with GWR Sutton Harbour branch at Friary Junction. From 1908, LSW loco. shed adjacent.

LYDD-ON-SEA HALT (4th July, 1937–6th March, 1967). A station until 1954. Between Greatstone and Lydd Town on New Romney re-aligned branch, 2¾m from Lydd Town. Sub-titled 'For Dungeness' though this was 2m away.

LYGHE HALT (1st September, 1911). Between Penshurst and Edenbridge on Redhill–Tonbridge line, 1¾m from former. Spelt Leigh until 1917, reverted to Leigh *c.*1960.

LYMINSTER HALT (1st August, 1907–September, 1914). Between Angmering and Ford Junction on West Coast line, 1m E of Arundel Junction. There was a station at Lyminster, called Littlehampton, from 1846, closed by 1863; this was on the opposite side of the LC from the Halt.

LYMPSTONE COMMANDO PLATFORM (March, 1976). Between Lympstone Halt and Exton (Woodbury Road) on Exmouth branch, 1m from Lympstone. For Royal Marines; restricted ('only persons having business at CTCRM may alight') but in public tables. This was built by Western Region.

M

MADDAFORD MOOR HALT (26th July, 1926–3rd October, 1966). Between Ashbury and Okehampton, 5m from latter, on Halwill line. Passing loop, two platforms.

MASBURY HALT (20th July, 1874–7th March, 1966). Between Binegar and Shepton Mallet near 'summit' on SDJ main line, 1¾m from Binegar. Station to 1938.

MEETH HALT (27th July, 1925–1st March, 1965). Between Hatherleigh and Petrockstowe on Torrington–Halwill line, 2¾m from Petrockstowe. Stone built; siding. (Meeth transfer siding for clay traffic was 1m N).

MELDON QUARRY STAFF HALT (*c.*1900–6th May, 1968). Between Okehampton and Bridestowe as main line passed within quarry area; for workers and wives. LSWR acquired the quarry in 1897.

MERTON PARK HALT. A station for most of its life, but appears as a halt on LBSC railmotor tickets for West Croydon–Wimbledon line, *c.*1919. May have related only to single 1870 Mitcham line platform, detached from the double-platform 1868 LBSC/LSW Joint station on Tooting Loop.

MEYRICK PARK HALT (1st March, 1906–October 1917). Between Bournemouth West and Central stations, halfway between Gasworks Junction and Central.

MIDDLE STOKE HALT (July, 1906–4th December, 1961). Between Beluncle Halt and Grain Crossing Halt on Port Victoria line, 3½m from Port Victoria. Situated S of Lower Stoke village, on track from Middle Stoke cottages.

MILTON RANGE HALT (July, 1906–17th September, 1932). Between Denton Halt and Hoo Junction on N. Kent line. For shooting parties; public to 17th July, 1932 but used after by special arrangement.

MILTON ROAD HALT (1906–1st May, 1915). Between Gravesend Central and Denton Halt, ½m from former.

MONKS LANE HALT (1st June, 1907–11th September, 1939). Between Hurst Green Junction and Edenbridge Town, 2m from latter. Situated on by-road ¾m N of Little Browns tunnel.

MORDEN ROAD HALT (*c*.1857). Former station, Morden Halt from *c*.1919, Morden Road Halt from 1938. Between Mitcham and Merton Park on W. Croydon–Wimbledon line. Single platform with SB; latter removed *c*.1960, small shelter added.

MOUNTFIELD HALT (1923–6th October, 1969). At Battle Road Crossing, between Robertsbridge and Battle, 3½m S of former. Still wooden sleeper platform, when closed. Ticket office in lean-to against LC keeper's house, across road from platforms.

MOUNT PLEASANT ROAD HALT (1906–2nd January, 1928). Between Lions Holt Halt and Exmouth Junction just E of Black Boy tunnel.

N

NANSTALLON HALT (2nd July, 1906–30th January, 1967). Between Dunmere Halt and Grogley Halt on Bodmin line, 2¼m from Bodmin. GWR 'pagoda' shelter. SC and siding.

NEW HYTHE HALT (9th December, 1929). Between Snodland and Aylesford on Maidstone line, 1½m from Snodland. Became a station 1936.

NORMANS BAY HALT (11th September, 1905). Between Pevensey Bay and Cooden Golf, 1¾m from former. Opened as Pevensey Sluice.

NUTBOURNE HALT (1st April, 1906). Between Southbourne Halt and Bosham on West Coast line, 1¾m from Bosham.

P

PARRACOMBE HALT (May, 1903–30th September, 1935). Between Woody Bay and Blackmoor on the narrow gauge Lynton & Barnstaple line. Loco water at Lynton end.

PAULSGROVE HALT (28th June, 1933–September, 1939). Between Cosham and Portchester for race meetings; two long narrow platforms behind grandstand.

PEVENSEY BAY HALT (11th September, 1905). On Eastbourne–St Leonards line, 2m E of Pevensey.

PILTON HALT (*c*.1900–1935). At Pilton Road Crossing, Barnstaple, on the narrow gauge Lynton line. In public tables to 1904, but mainly for railwaymen at Pilton Yard.

POLSHAM HALT (December 1861–29th October, 1951). On SDJR between Wells and Glastonbury; former station.

POLSLOE BRIDGE HALT (1907). Between Exmouth Junction and Topsham on Exmouth line. Full length platforms (2); down line lifted 1973.

PURLEY DOWNS GOLF COURSE HALT (*c*.1914–1927). Between Sanderstead and Riddlesdown on the Oxted line. Proof of existence not entirely satisfactory but recalled locally.

R

REEDHAM HALT (1st March, 1911). Between Purley and Smitham, ¾m from latter, later (*c*.1932) a station.

RICHBOROUGH CASTLE HALT (29th June, 1918–11th September, 1939). Between Sandwich and Minster, for military. Public from 19th June, 1933.

RIDHAM HALT: see Swale Halt.

ROFFEY ROAD HALT (1st June, 1907–3rd January, 1937). Between Faygate and Littlehaven Halt on Three Bridges-Horsham line, ¾m from Faygate. On by-road just off Crawley–Horsham road.

ROSHERVILLE HALT (10th May, 1886–16th July, 1933). Former station, ½m from Gravesend West Street. A halt from 1928. Island platform.

ROUNDBALL HALT (1909–1920). Between Honiton and Sidmouth Junction, ½m W of Honiton, for rifle-range. On by-road from Brownhill to Honiton Station.

ROWAN HALT (18th December, 1933–1st January, 1939). Near foot of Dyke branch, for housing estate. No loop, but some push-pull trains from Brighton terminated here.

RUSPER ROAD CROSSING HALT: see Littlehaven Halt.

Waddon Marsh Halt, showing its location inside the gasworks area. *Lens of Sutton*

Fishbourne Halt. *Lens of Sutton*

S

ST JAMES' PARK HALT: see Lions Holt Halt.

ST LAWRENCE HALT (20th July, 1897–15th September, 1952). Station until 1927; between Ventnor West and Whitwell; single platform, large SB.

SALFORDS HALT (8th October, 1915). Between Earlswood and Horley on main line, 2m from Earlswood, for workers at Monotype factory. New halt built 17th July, 1932, made a station 1st January, 1935. Salfords Goods Depot adjacent.

SANDHURST HALT (1909). Between Blackwater and Crowthorne on Guildford–Reading line, 1¼m from Blackwater.

SANDSFOOT CASTLE HALT (1st August, 1932–3rd March, 1952). Between Rodwell and Wyke Regis Halt on Portland line, ¾m from Rodwell. Timber platform; wire fence along centre with footpaths to castle etc. at rear.

SEVEN STONES HALT (June 1910–1917). On former PDSWJ Callington line between Latchley and Luckett, ½m N of former. At request of mine owner, Clitters United. Stone, no shelter. Possibly called Phoenix Mine when opened.

SHAKESPEARE CLIFF STAFF HALT (2nd June, 1913–?). Between Warren Halt and Dover, used by miners 1913–20, Navy 1920, military 1941, workmen for Channel Tunnel 1973, railwaymen after. Located just W of tunnel.

SHOOTING RANGE PLATFORM (*c.*1885–1947). Between Grogley Halt and Wadebridge, 1½m from latter. Not in tables.

SHOREHAM AIRPORT HALT: see Bungalow Town Halt.

SHOSCOMBE & SINGLE HILL HALT (23rd September, 1929–7th March, 1966). On SDJR between Wellow and Radstock, 1¾m from former.

SINDLESHAM HALT: see Winnersh Halt.

SNAILHAM HALT (1st July, 1907–2nd February, 1959). Between Doleham Halt and Winchelsea, 1½m from latter; opened as Snailham Crossing Halt.

SNAPPER HALT (*c.*1903–30th September, 1935). On narrow gauge Lynton line, between Barnstaple and Chelfham, 2¾m from former. Low ash platform, rendered brick shelter. At closing, brake compo. 6991 left on rails near shelter, 3rd brake 6993 ditto a few yards N of halt.

SNOWDOWN & NONINGTON HALT (1914). Between Aylesham Halt and Shepherdswell on main line, 2m from latter, mainly for colliery workers. SC; sidings each end.

SOUTHBOURNE HALT (1st April, 1906). Between Nutbourne Halt and Emsworth on West Coast line, 1½m from Emsworth.

SOUTHEASE & RODMELL HALT (1st September, 1906). On Seaford branch, between Lewes and Newhaven, 3½m from former. SC on other side of crossing carried name 'Itford Crossing' until *c.*1960. Concrete FB later.

SOUTH STREET HALT (1st June, 1911–1st January, 1931). On Canterbury–Whitstable line between Tankerton Halt and Blean Halt, ¾m from former.

SPENCER ROAD HALT (1st September, 1906–15th March, 1915). On Woodside & South Croydon Railway (joint LBSC/SECR), half-way between Coombe Lane and Selsdon Road.

SPETISBURY HALT (1st November, 1860–17th September, 1956). On SDJR between Charlton Marshall Halt and Bailey Gate, 3m from latter. Originally single-platform station, doubled later, reduced to halt 1939. Located on side-road NW of village.

STOKE JUNCTION HALT (17th July, 1932–4th December, 1961). Between Middle Stoke Halt and Port Victoria, at junction with Allhallows branch. Originally a siding; ground level SC 1932.

STONE CROSS HALT (11th September, 1905–7th July, 1935). Between Pevensey and Hampden Park, 1½m from former; located at crossing of Hailsham–Eastbourne Road.

STONE CROSSING HALT (2nd November, 1908). Between Dartford and Greenhithe on N. Kent line, 2m from former. Ground level SC. From 1919 had exchange siding with APCM Kent Works railway.

STONEHALL & LYDDEN HALT (1914–5th April, 1954). Between Shepherdswell and Kearsney on main line, 1½m from Kearsney. Located on by-road N of A2, 1m E of Lydden village.

STOURPAINE & DURWESTON HALT (9th July, 1928–17th September, 1956). Between Shillingstone and Blandford on SDJR, 1½m N of Blandford.

SWALE HALT (1913). On Sheerness branch at crossing of R. Swale. Originally a staff halt, possibly called Ridham Dock. Became public from December 1922 when a ship collision put the bridge out of action; halt also set up on N side of Swale during the time bridge was closed, to 1st November, 1923, when N halt closed, S halt named Kings Ferry Bridge Halt; renamed Swale Halt 1929. Bridge re-aligned and new halt opened 20th April, 1960, with road on down side, instead of up side as before.

SWANSCOMBE HALT (2nd November, 1908). Between Greenhithe and Northfleet on N. Kent line, originally 1m from latter, near Craylands Road. Abandoned and new halt built ¼m east 6th July, 1930 (SR tables continued to give wrong mileage for 30 years).

T

TANKERTON HALT (1st July, 1914–1st January, 1931). Between Whitstable Harbour and South Street Halt, ¾m from former, at point where branch goes under LCD main line. To make connections with re-sited Whitstable & Tankerton station (1915) to which a footpath ran.

TESTON CROSSING HALT (1st September, 1909–2nd November, 1959). Between Wateringbury and East Farleigh, 1m from former, on Paddock Wood–Maidstone line.

THREE OAKS & GUESTLING HALT (1st July, 1907). Between Doleham Halt and Ore on Rye–Hastings line, 2¾m from latter. Opened as Three Oaks Bridge. Situated against overbridge on Copsall–Coghurst lane.

TRELOARS HOSPITAL PLATFORM (*c.*1918–1939). On branch from Alton. Also called Cripples Home Siding.

TYLER HILL HALT: see Blean.

U

UPPER HALLIFORD HALT (1st May, 1944). Between Sunbury and Shepperton ¾m from former; opened as Halliford Halt.

URALITE HALT (July, 1906–4th December, 1961). Between Denton Halt and Cliffe on Port Victoria line, just beyond Hoo Junction. Siding to British Uralite Works.

W

WADDON MARSH HALT (6th July, 1930). Between Beddington Lane Halt and West Croydon, 1¼m from latter. Island platform, concrete FB. SC, and goods lines both sides; adjacent to Croydon Gasworks.

WARBLINGTON HALT (1st November, 1907). Between Emsworth and Havant, ½m from latter. Opened as Denville Halt.

WARREN HALT (1st June, 1908–*c.*1970). Between Folkestone Junction and Shakespeare Cliff Halt, 1m E of former. Public to 25th September, 1939. Closed by landslide 19th December, 1915–August, 1919. No service shown in 'thirties but used by railwaymen, probably to 1951, after official closing. Wooden FB, small ticket office.

Greatstone-on-Sea Halt. *Lens of Sutton*

Stoke Junction Halt. *Lens of Sutton*

WATCHINGWELL HALT (20th July, 1888–21st September, 1953). Former private station between Carisbrooke and Calbourne on FYN (IOW). In public tables from 1923, became a halt 1948. Solid platform, brick SB.

WATERGATE HALT (20th September, 1926–1st March, 1965). Between Yarde Halt and Torrington on Halwill line, 1¾m from Torrington. Siding and GF on opposite side of road crossing.

WEST BEXHILL HALT: see Collington Halt.

WESTCOTT RANGE HALT (November, 1916–*c.*1928). Between Gomshall and Dorking Town, 1½m from latter.

WESTHAM HALT (1st July, 1909–3rd March, 1952). On Portland branch between Melcombe Regis and Rodwell, ½m from former, on Abbotsbury Road, at Littlefield Crossing.

WESTON MILL HALT (1st November, 1906–14th September, 1921). Between Camels Head Halt and St Budeaux, ¼m from latter, at Bridewell Road.

WHIPTON BRIDGE HALT (March, 1906–1st January, 1923). Between Exmouth Junction and Pinhoe, 1m from latter, on Honiton line.

WHITWELL HALT (20th July, 1897–15th September, 1952). Former station between St Lawrence and Godshill on Ventnor West branch, IOW. A halt from 1941.

WIMBLEDON STAFF HALT (*c.*1915). Between Earlsfield and Wimbledon, adjacent to Durnsford Road electrical depot.

WINCHELSEA HALT (13th February, 1851). Former station between Rye and Doleham Halt; double platform station replaced by single platform with iron shelter.

WINCHESTER TROOP PLATFORM (November, 1918–1919). Between Micheldever and Winchester City, ¾m N of latter. Not public.

WINNERSH HALT (1st January, 1910). Between Wokingham and Earley, 2m from latter, on Reading–Guildford line. Sindlesham & Hurst Halt until 1930.

WOODCROFT HALT (4th October, 1943–1st October, 1945). Between Petersfield and Rowlands Castle, ½m E of Chalton Village, for naval base. Also called Ditcham Park Halt.

WOODSFORD HALT (*c.*1920–1929). Between Moreton and Dorchester for army, situated near crossing of Higher Woodsford–Overmoyne road.

WYKE REGIS HALT (1st July, 1909–3rd March, 1952). Between Portland and Rodwell on Easton line, 2m from Portland, near Torpedo Works. Joint LSW/GW.

Knowle Halt; the right-hand line passes through the tunnel, the other two by-passing it. *Lens of Sutton*

Yarde Halt. *Lens of Sutton*

YARDE HALT (19th July, 1926–1st March, 1965). Between Watergate Halt and Dunsbear Halt on Torrington–Halwill line.

The total number of halts opened was as follows:

By the	LSWR	26	LBSC/LSW Joint	2
	LBSC	29	SECR/LBSC Joint	2
	SECR	35	Somerset & Dorset	5
	SR	23	Lynton & Barnstaple	4
	BR(S)	4	LSW/SR/GW Joint	5
			Stations converted to halts	19

Grand total 154

High Halstow Halt. *Lens of Sutton*

DUNTON GREEN, BRASTED, and WESTERHAM.

Miles from Dunton Green	Down.	Week Days. mrn	mrn	mrn	mrn	mrn	mrn	mrn S	mrn E	aft S	aft E	aft S	aft E	aft S	aft E	aft S	aft E	aft	aft E
	340 Charing Cross ....dep.	..	..	7 24	8 5	..	..	..	1153	–	1236	..	..	..	..	3 0	3 25	4A30	5 15
	340 Waterloo Junction "	...	...	7 26	8 7	...	...	...	1155	...	1238	...	...	...	...	...	3 28	4B32	...
	340 Cannon Street "	5 10	..	..	..	9 12	..	1133	..	1230	1240	1 21	..	2 10	..	3 9	..	4 33	..
	340 London Bridge "	5 30	...	7 33	8 16	9 18	...	1138	12 2	1234	1245	1 24	...	2 12	...	3 12	3 35	4 37	5 22
	Dunton Green ....dep.	6 35	7 20	8 18	9 2	1010	11 0	1225	1245	1 18	1 30	2 6	2 32	3 5	3 35	4 7	4 22	5 20	5 56
1¼	Chevening Halt	6 38	7 23	..	9 5	1013	11 3	1228	1248	1 21	1 33	2 9	2 35	3 8	3 38	4 10	4 25	5 23	5 59
3¼	Brasted	6 43	7 28	8 22	9 10	1018	11 8	1233	1253	1 26	1 38	2 14	2 40	3 13	3 43	4 15	4 30	5 28	6 4
4¾	Westerham ....arr.	6 48	7 33	8 30	9 15	1023	1113	1238	1258	1 31	1 43	2 19	2 45	3 18	3 48	4 20	4 35	5 33	6 9

Down.	Week Days—Continued. aft	aft	aft	aft	aft N	aft N	Sundays. mrn	mrn	mrn	mrn	aft	aft	aft	aft	aft	aft	aft
340 Charing Cross ....dep.	5 30	6 30	7 40	9 30	1035	1146	6 20	9 1	10 1	1143	3 30	..	5 35	6 35	..	8 1	10 1
340 Waterloo Junction "	5 32	6 32	7 42	9 32	1037	...	...	9 3	10 3	1145	3 32	...	5 38	6 37	...	8 3	10 3
340 Cannon Street "	..	..	..	..	..	..	..	9 5	10 5	..	..	..	..	..	..	..	..
340 London Bridge "	5 37	6 37	7 48	9 39	1041	...	6 37	9 9	10 9	1151	3 40	...	5 46	6 43	...	8 6	10 6
Dunton Green ....dep.	6 24	7 24	8 28	1020	1127	1230	7 40	1016	1055	1239	4 17	5 35	6 35	7 25	8 5	8 56	1055
Chevening Halt	6 27	7 27	8 31	1023	1131	1233	7 43	1021	1058	1242	4 22	5 38	6 38	7 28	8 8	8 59	11 0
Brasted	6 32	7 32	8 36	1029	1136	1239	7 48	1026	11 3	1247	4 27	5 43	6 43	7 33	8 13	9 4	11 5
Westerham ....arr.	6 37	7 37	8 41	1034	1141	1244	7 53	1031	11 8	1252	4 32	5 48	6 48	7 38	8 18	9 9	1110

Miles	Up.	Week Days. mrn	mrn	mrn	mrn	mrn	mrn S	mrn E	non	aft S	aft E	aft S	aft E	aft S	aft E	aft S	aft E	aft	aft E
	Westerham ....dep.	6 3	7 2	7 38	8 38	9 48	1035	1040	12 0	1255	1 3	1 37	2 14	2 45	3 15	3 40	3 57	4 52	5 38
1½	Brasted	6 7	7 6	7 42	8 42	9 52	1039	1044	12 4	1259	1 7	1 41	2 18	2 49	3 19	3 44	4 1	4 56	5 42
3½	Chevening Halt	6 12	7 11	7 47	8 47	9 57	1044	1049	12 9	1 4	1 12	1 46	2 23	2 54	3 24	3 49	4 6	5 1	5 47
4¾	Dunton Green 322, 343 ..arr.	6 16	7 15	7 51	8 50	10 1	1048	1053	1213	1 8	1 16	1 50	2 27	2 58	3 28	3 53	4 10	5 5	5 51
23¾	343 London Bridge ....arr.	7 18	8 7	8 32	9 32	1046	1129	1135	1255	1 56	1 55	2 50	3 9	..	4 8	4 35	5 9	6F6	..
24	343 Cannon Street "	...	...	8 36	9 36	...	1135	1141	1 0	...	...	2 53	3 17	...	4 13	4 40	...	6J32	...
24¾	343 Waterloo Junction "	7 22	8 12	8 49	..	1052	..	..	1H21	2 1	2 1	2 58	..	..	4 18	4 39	5 13	6K10	..
25¼	343 Charing Cross "	7 25	8 16	8 52	...	1056	...	...	1L24	2 5	2 5	3 2	...	...	4 21	4 42	5 16	6H18	...

Up.	Week Days—Continued. aft S	aft	aft	aft	aft N	ngt N	Sundays. mrn	mrn	mrn	aft	aft	aft	aft	aft	aft	aft	aft
Westerham ....dep.	6 5	7 0	8 10	9 40	1038	12 5	7 18	8 23	1036	1220	1 30	5 13	6 13	7 6	7 43	8 23	9 23
Brasted	6 9	7 4	8 14	9 44	1042	12 9	7 22	8 27	1040	1224	1 34	5 17	6 17	7 10	7 47	8 27	9 27
Chevening Halt	6 14	7 9	8 19	9 49	1047	1214	7 27	8 32	1045	1229	1 39	5 22	6 22	7 15	7 52	8 32	9 32
Dunton Green 322, 343 ....arr.	6 18	7 13	8 23	9 53	1051	1218	7 31	8 36	1049	1233	1 42	5 26	6 26	7 19	7 56	8 36	9 35
343 London Bridge ....arr.	..	7 59	..	1037	1132	..	..	9 26	1153	..	2 31	6 10	..	8 13	8 43	9 15	1031
343 Cannon Street "	...	...	...	...	...	...	...	...	...	...	...	6 14	...	...	...	...	...
343 Waterloo Junction "	..	8 6	..	1041	1139	..	..	9 33	1159	..	2 34	6 34	..	8 18	8 48	9 21	1034
343 Charing Cross "	...	8 10	..	1044	1143	...	...	9 37	12 8	...	2 37	6 37	...	8 22	8 52	9 25	1037

A Dep 4 18 aft. on Sats. B Dep 4 20 aft. on Sats. E or E Except Sats. F Arr 5 46 aft on Sats. H Arr 1 10 aft. on Sats. J Arr 6 19 aft. on Sats. K Arr 5 52 aft. on Sats. L Arr 1 13 aft. on Sats. N Weds. only. H Arr 5 56 aft. on Sats. S or S Sats. only.

GRAVESEND CENTRAL and PORT VICTORIA.

Miles	Down.	Week Days. mrn	mrn	mrn	mrn	aft	aft S	aft E	aft S	aft E	aft S	Sundays. mrn	mrn	aft
	Gravesend Central ....dep.	5 50	6 45	8 12	1037	2 13	5 23	5 35	7 54	8 4	9 40	7 0	1115	6 15
1	Denton Halt	...	6 47	8 14	1040	2 16	...	...	...	...	9 42	7 2	1117	6 17
2¼	Milton Range Halt	..	..	..	Aa	..	..	..	..	..	..	Aa	Aa	..
3¾	Uralite Halt	...	6 53	8 21	1048	2 25	5 30	5 43	8 1	8 11	...	7 9	1121	6 24
6	Cliffe	..	6 58	8 26	1053	2 30	5 35	5 48	8 6	8 16	9 53	7 14	1129	6 29
8¼	High Halstow Halt	...	7 5	8 33	11 0	2 37	5 42	5 55	8 13	8 23	10 0	7 21	1136	6 36
9	Sharnal Street C	6 8	7 8	8 36	11 8	2 40	5 45	5 58	8 17	8 27	10 8	7 24	1139	6 39
10¼	Beluncle Halt	...	7 11	8 39	11 7	2 45	5 50	6 1	8 20	8 30	10 6	7 27	1142	6 42
12¼	Middle Stoke Halt	..	7 16	8 44	1112	2 50	5 55	6 6	8 25	8 35	1011	7 32	1147	6 47
14¼	Grain Crossing Halt	...	7 21	8 49	1117	2 55	6 0	6 11	8 30	8 40	1016	7 37	1152	6 52
16	Port Victoria ....arr.	..	7 25	8 53	1121	3 0	6 4	6 15	8 35	8 45	1020	7 41	1156	6 56

Miles	Up.	Week Days. mrn	mrn	mrn	aft S	aft E	aft	aft E	aft S	aft	aft S	Sundays. mrn	aft	aft
	Port Victoria ....dep.	..	7 40	9 0	1255	1 14	3 24	5 5	6 20	9 8	1040	7 56	1256	7 5
1¼	Grain Crossing Halt	...	7 43	9 3	1258	1 17	3 27	5 8	6 23	9 11	...	7 59	1259	7 8
3¼	Middle Stoke Halt	..	7 48	9 8	1 3	1 22	3 32	5 13	6 28	9 16	..	8 4	1 4	7 13
5¼	Beluncle Halt	...	7 55	9 13	1 8	1 27	3 37	5 18	6 33	9 22	...	8 10	1 9	7 19
6¾	Sharnal Street C	6 16	7 58	9 16	1 11	1 30	3 40	5 21	6 36	9 25	1055	8 13	1 12	7 22
7¾	High Halstow Halt	6 18	8 2	9 19	1 14	1 33	3 44	5 24	6 39	9 29	1058	8 16	1 15	7 25
10	Cliffe	6 25	8 9	9 26	1 21	1 40	3 51	5 31	6 46	9 36	11 5	8 23	1 22	7 32
12¼	Uralite Halt	6 30	8 14	9 30	1 26	1 45	3 56	5 35	6 51	...	...	8 28	1 27	7 37
13¾	Milton Range Halt	..	..	Aa	Aa	Aa	..	..	..	..	..	Aa	Aa	..
15	Denton Halt	...	...	9 38	1 33	1 52	4 3	5 40	6 58	...	...	8 36	1 35	7 45
16	Gravesend Cen. 348, 359 arr.	6 39	8 26	9 42	1 37	1 56	4 7	5 44	7 2	9 50	1119	8 40	1 39	7 49

Aa Stops on informing the Guard. C Sta. for Hoo and St. Mary's Hoo (2 mls.). E Except Sats. S Sats. only.

Bradshaw's Timetable of January 1931.

⊖—All Trains on this page are Third class only

Table 67

Table 67 — WEST CROYDON, MITCHAM and WIMBLEDON ⊖

Miles	Down	Mondays to Fridays																																			
		am	am	am	am	am	am	am	am	am	am	am	am	am	am	am		pm	pm		pm	pm	pm	pm	pm	pm	pm	pm	pm	pm	pm	pm	pm	pm	pm	pm	pm
	West Croydon dep	6 31	6 51	7 11	7 31	7 51	8 11	8 31	8 51	9 11	9 31	9 51	1011	1044	1114	1144	..	1214	1244	..	1 14	1 44	2 14	2 44	3 14	3 45	4 9	4 30	4 52	5 12	5 31	5 51	6 11	6 31	6 51	7 11	7 31
1¼	Waddon Marsh Halt	6 34	6 54	7 14	7 34	7 54	8 14	8 34	8 54	9 14	9 34	9 54	1014	1047	1117	1147	....	1217	1247	....	1 17	1 47	2 17	2 47	3 17	3 48	4 12	4 33	4 55	5 15	5 34	5 54	6 14	6 34	6 54	7 14	7 34
2½	Beddington Lane Halt	6 37	6 57	7 17	7 37	7 57	8 17	8 37	8 57	9 17	9 37	9 57	1017	1050	1120	1150	..	1220	1250	..	1 20	1 50	2 20	2 50	3 20	3 51	4 15	4 36	4 58	5 18	5 37	5 57	6 17	6 37	6 57	7 17	7 37
3½	Mitcham Junction	6 39	6 59	7 19	7 39	7 59	8 19	8 39	8 59	9 19	9 39	9 59	1019	1052	1122	1152	....	1222	1252	....	1 22	1 52	2 22	2 52	3 22	3 53	4 17	4 39	5 0	5 20	5 39	5 59	6 19	6 39	6 59	7 19	7 39
3¾	Mitcham	6 41	7 1	7 21	7 41	8 1	8 21	8 41	9 1	9 21	9 41	10 1	1021	1054	1124	1154	..	1224	1254	..	1 24	1 54	2 24	2 54	3 24	3 58	4 19	4 41	5 2	5 22	5 41	6 1	6 21	6 41	7 1	7 21	7 41
5	Morden Road Halt	6 44	7 4	7 24	7 44	8 4	8 24	8 44	9 4	9 24	9 44	10 4	1024	1057	1127	1157	....	1227	1257	....	1 27	1 57	2 27	2 57	3 27	4 1	4 21	4 44	5 5	5 25	5 44	6 4	6 24	6 44	7 4	7 24	7 44
5½	Merton Park	6 46	7 6	7 26	7 46	8 6	8 26	8 46	9 6	9 26	9 46	10 6	1026	1059	1129	1159	..	1229	1259	..	1 29	1 59	2 29	2 59	3 29	4 3	4 26	4 45	5 7	5 26	5 46	6 6	6 26	6 46	7 6	7 26	7 46
6¼	**Wimbledon** arr	6 49	7 9	7 29	7 49	8 9	8 29	8 48	9 9	9 28	9 48	10 9	1029	11 1	1131	12 1	....	1231	1 1	....	1 31	2 1	2 31	3 1	3 31	4 6	4 29	4 48	5 9	5 29	5 49	6 9	6 29	6 49	7 9	7 29	7 49

Down	Mondays to Fridays—cont.									Saturdays																												
	pm	pm	pm	pm	pm	pm	pm			am	am	am	am	am	am	am	am	am	am	am	am	am		am	am		am		pm	pm	pm	pm	pm	pm		pm	pm
West Croydon dep	7 52	8 14	8 44	9 19	9 44	1019	1044	..	..	6 31	6 51	7 11	7 31	7 51	8 11	8 31	8 51	9 11	9 31	9 51	1011	1046	..	1111	1131	..	1151	..	1211	1231	1251	1 11	1 31	1 51	..	2 11	2 31
Waddon Marsh Halt	7 55	8 17	8 47	9 22	9 47	1022	1047	....	....	6 34	6 54	7 14	7 34	7 54	8 14	8 34	8 54	9 14	9 34	9 54	1014	1049	....	1114	1134	....	1154	....	1214	1234	1254	1 14	1 34	1 54	....	2 14	2 34
Beddington Lane Halt	7 58	8 20	8 50	9 25	9 50	1025	1050	..	..	6 37	6 57	7 17	7 37	7 57	8 17	8 37	8 57	9 17	9 37	9 57	1017	1052	..	1117	1137	..	1157	..	1217	1237	1257	1 17	1 37	1 57	..	2 17	2 37
Mitcham Junction	8 0	8 22	8 52	9 27	9 52	1027	1052	....	....	6 39	6 59	7 19	7 39	7 59	8 19	8 39	8 59	9 19	9 39	9 59	1019	1054	....	1119	1139	....	1159	....	1219	1239	1259	1 19	1 39	1 59	....	2 19	2 39
Mitcham	8 2	8 26	8 54	9 29	9 54	1029	1054	..	..	6 41	7 1	7 21	7 41	8 1	8 21	8 41	9 1	9 21	9 41	10 1	1021	1056	..	1121	1141	..	12 1	..	1221	1241	1 1	1 21	1 41	2 1	..	2 21	2 41
Morden Road Halt	8 4	8 28	8 57	9 32	9 57	1032	1057	....	....	6 44	7 4	7 24	7 44	8 4	8 24	8 44	9 4	9 24	9 44	10 4	1024	1059	....	1124	1144	....	12 4	....	1224	1244	1 4	1 24	1 44	2 4	....	2 24	2 44
Merton Park	8 6	8 30	8 59	9 34	9 59	1034	1059	..	..	6 46	7 6	7 26	7 46	8 6	8 26	8 46	9 6	9 26	9 46	10 6	1026	11 1	..	1126	1146	..	12 6	..	1226	1246	1 6	1 26	1 46	2 6	..	2 26	2 46
Wimbledon arr	8 9	8 33	9 1	9 36	10 1	1036	11 1	....	....	6 49	7 9	7 29	7 49	8 9	8 29	8 48	9 9	9 28	9 48	10 9	1029	11 3	....	1129	1149	....	12 9	....	1229	1249	1 9	1 29	1 49	2 9	....	2 29	2 49

Down	Saturdays—continued																	Sundays															
	pm	pm	pm	pm	pm	pm	pm	pm	pm	pm	pm	pm	pm	pm	pm	pm	pm		am	am		am	am		am (Repeat each hour until 7 14 pm)	am (Repeat each hour until 7 44 pm)		pm		pm	pm	pm		
West Croydon dep	2 51	3 14	3 44	4 13	4 42	5 14	5 41	6 14	6 44	7 13	7 48	8 14	8 44	9 19	9 44	1019	1044	..	7 8	7 47	..	8 18	8 44	..	9 14	9 44	..	8 14	..	8 44	9 14	9 44	..	..
Waddon Marsh Halt	2 54	3 17	3 47	4 16	4 45	5 17	5 44	6 17	6 47	7 16	7 51	8 17	8 47	9 22	9 47	1022	1047	....	7 11	7 50	....	8 21	8 47	....	9 17	9 47	....	9 17	....	8 47	9 17	9 47	....	....
Beddington Lane Halt	2 57	3 20	3 50	4 19	4 48	5 20	5 47	6 20	6 50	7 19	7 54	8 20	8 50	9 25	9 50	1025	1050	..	7 14	7 53	..	8 24	8 51	..	9 21	9 50	..	8 21	..	8 50	9 21	9 50	..	..
Mitcham Junction	2 59	3 22	3 52	4 21	4 50	5 22	5 49	6 22	6 52	7 21	7 56	8 22	8 52	9 27	9 52	1027	1052	....	7 15	7 55	....	8 26	8 53	....	9 23	9 52	....	8 23	....	8 52	9 23	9 52	....	....
Mitcham	3 1	3 24	3 54	4 23	4 52	5 24	5 51	6 24	6 54	7 23	7 58	8 26	8 54	9 29	9 54	1029	1054	..	7 18	7 57	..	8 28	8 55	..	9 25	9 54	..	8 25	..	8 54	9 25	9 54	..	..
Morden Road Halt	3 4	3 27	3 57	4 26	4 54	5 27	5 54	6 27	6 57	7 26	8 0	8 28	8 57	9 32	9 57	1032	1057	....	7 20	8 0	....	8 31	8 58	....	9 28	9 57	....	9 28	....	8 57	9 28	9 57	....	....
Merton Park	3 6	3 29	3 59	4 28	4 56	5 29	5 56	6 29	6 59	7 28	8 2	8 30	8 59	9 34	9 59	1034	1059	..	7 23	8 2	..	8 33	9 0	..	9 30	9 59	..	8 30	..	8 59	9 30	9 59	..	..
Wimbledon arr	3 8	3 31	4 1	4 30	4 59	5 31	5 58	6 31	7 1	7 30	8 5	8 33	9 1	9 36	10 1	1036	11 1	....	7 25	8 5	....	8 36	9 2	....	9 32	10 2	....	8 32	....	9 2	9 32	10 2	....	....

Miles	Up	Mondays to Fridays																																		
		am	am	am	am	am	am	am	am	am	am	am	am	am	am	am		pm	pm	pm	pm	pm	pm	pm	pm	pm	pm	pm	pm	pm		pm	pm	pm	pm	pm	pm
	Wimbledon dep	6 31	6 52	7 12	7 32	7 52	8 12	8 32	8 52	9 12	9 32	9 52	1012	1046	1117	1145	..	1217	1246	1 15	1 46	2 17	2 45	3 15	3 48	4 10	4 32	4 53	5 12	5 32	..	5 52	6 12	6 32	6 52	7 12	7 32
¾	Merton Park	6 33	6 54	7 14	7 34	7 54	8 14	8 34	8 54	9 14	9 34	9 54	1014	1048	1119	1147	....	1219	1248	1 17	1 48	2 19	2 47	3 17	3 50	4 12	4 34	4 55	5 14	5 34	....	5 54	6 14	6 34	6 54	7 14	7 34
1¼	Morden Road Halt	6 35	6 55	7 15	7 35	7 55	8 15	8 35	8 55	9 15	9 35	9 56	1015	1049	1120	1148	..	1220	1249	1 19	1 49	2 21	2 48	3 19	3 51	4 14	4 35	4 57	5 16	5 35	..	5 55	6 15	6 35	6 55	7 15	7 35
2½	Mitcham	6 38	6 58	7 18	7 38	7 58	8 18	8 38	8 58	9 18	9 38	9 58	1018	1052	1123	1151	....	1226	1252	1 21	1 52	2 23	2 51	3 21	3 54	4 16	4 38	4 59	5 19	5 38	....	5 58	6 18	6 38	6 58	7 18	7 38
3	Mitcham Junction	6 40	7 0	7 20	7 40	8 0	8 20	8 40	9 0	9 20	9 40	10 0	1020	1054	1125	1153	..	1228	1254	1 23	1 54	2 25	2 53	3 23	3 56	4 18	4 40	5 1	5 21	5 40	..	6 0	6 20	6 40	7 0	7 20	7 40
3¾	Beddington Lane Halt	6 42	7 2	7 22	7 42	8 2	8 22	8 42	9 2	9 22	9 42	10 2	1022	1056	1127	1155	....	1230	1256	1 25	1 56	2 27	2 55	3 25	3 58	4 20	4 42	5 3	5 23	5 42	....	6 2	6 22	6 42	7 2	7 22	7 42
5	Waddon Marsh Halt	6 45	7 5	7 25	7 45	8 5	8 25	8 45	9 5	9 25	9 45	10 5	1025	1059	1130	1158	..	1233	1259	1 28	1 59	2 30	2 58	3 28	4 1	4 23	4 45	5 6	5 26	5 45	..	6 5	6 25	6 45	7 5	7 25	7 45
6¼	**West Croydon** arr	6 49	7 9	7 29	7 49	8 9	8 29	8 49	9 9	9 29	9 49	10 9	1029	11 3	1134	12 2	....	1237	1 3	1 32	2 3	2 34	3 2	3 32	4 5	4 27	4 49	5 10	5 29	5 49	....	6 9	6 29	6 49	7 9	7 29	7 49

Up	Mondays to Fridays—continued										Saturdays																											
	pm	pm	pm		pm	pm	pm	pm			am	am		am	am	am	am		am	am	am	am		am	am	am	am		am	am		am	am	am	am	am	am
Wimbledon dep	7 52	8 18	8 43	..	9 20	9 45	1020	1045	..	..	6 31	6 52	..	7 12	7 32	7 52	8 12	..	8 32	8 52	9 12	9 32	..	9 52	1012	1047	1112	..	1132	1152	..	1212	1232	1252	1 12	1 32	1 52
Merton Park	7 54	8 20	8 45	....	9 22	9 47	1022	1047	....	....	6 33	6 54	....	7 14	7 34	7 54	8 14	....	8 34	8 54	9 14	9 34	....	9 54	1014	1049	1114	....	1134	1154	....	1214	1234	1254	1 14	1 34	1 54
Morden Road Halt	7 55	8 22	8 47	..	9 24	9 48	1024	1049	..	..	6 35	6 55	..	7 15	7 35	7 55	8 15	..	8 35	8 55	9 15	9 35	..	9 56	1015	1050	1115	..	1135	1155	..	1215	1235	1255	1 15	1 35	1 55
Mitcham	7 59	8 25	8 50	....	9 26	9 51	1026	1051	....	....	6 38	6 58	....	7 18	7 38	7 58	8 18	....	8 38	8 58	9 18	9 38	....	9 58	1018	1053	1118	....	1138	1158	....	1218	1238	1258	1 18	1 38	1 58
Mitcham Junction	8 1	8 27	8 53	..	9 28	9 53	1028	1053	..	..	6 40	7 0	..	7 20	7 40	8 0	8 20	..	8 40	9 0	9 20	9 40	..	10 0	1020	1055	1120	..	1140	12 0	..	1220	1240	1 0	1 20	1 40	2 0
Beddington Lane Halt	8 3	8 29	8 55	....	9 30	9 55	1030	1055	....	....	6 42	7 2	....	7 22	7 42	8 2	8 22	....	8 42	9 2	9 22	9 42	....	10 2	1022	1057	1122	....	1142	12 2	....	1222	1242	1 2	1 22	1 42	2 2
Waddon Marsh Halt	8 6	8 32	8 58	..	9 33	9 58	1033	1058	..	..	6 45	7 5	..	7 25	7 45	8 5	8 25	..	8 45	9 5	9 25	9 45	..	10 5	1025	11 0	1125	..	1145	12 5	..	1225	1245	1 5	1 25	1 45	2 5
West Croydon arr	8 9	8 36	9 2	....	9 37	10 2	1037	11 2	....	....	6 49	7 9	....	7 29	7 49	8 9	8 29	....	8 49	9 9	9 29	9 49	....	10 9	1029	11 4	1129	....	1149	12 9	....	1229	1249	1 9	1 29	1 49	2 9

Up	Saturdays—continued																										Sundays								
	pm	pm	pm	pm		pm		pm	pm	pm		pm	pm	pm		pm	pm	pm	pm	pm		pm	pm	pm			am		am		am	am		am (Repeat each hour until 9 15 pm)	am (Repeat each hour until 9 45 pm)
Wimbledon dep	2 12	2 32	2 52	3 15	..	3 45	..	4 15	4 42	5 15	..	5 42	6 15	6 45	..	7 14	7 48	8 18	8 43	9 20	..	9 45	1020	1045	..	..	7 28	..	7 49	..	8 7	8 45	..	9 15	9 45
Merton Park	2 14	2 34	2 54	3 17	....	3 47	....	4 17	4 44	5 17	....	5 44	6 17	6 47	....	7 16	7 50	8 20	8 45	9 22	....	9 47	1022	1047	....	....	7 30	....	7 51	....	8 9	8 47	....	9 17	9 47
Morden Road Halt	2 15	2 35	2 56	3 18	..	3 49	..	4 18	4 46	5 18	..	5 46	6 18	6 49	..	7 17	7 52	8 22	8 47	9 24	..	9 48	1024	1049	..	..	7 32	..	7 52	..	8 10	8 48	..	9 18	9 48
Mitcham	2 18	2 38	2 58	3 21	....	3 51	....	4 21	4 48	5 21	....	5 48	6 21	6 51	....	7 20	7 55	8 25	8 50	9 26	....	9 51	1026	1051	....	....	7 35	....	7 55	....	8 13	8 52	....	9 22	9 51
Mitcham Junction	2 20	2 40	3 0	3 23	..	3 53	..	4 23	4 51	5 23	..	5 50	6 23	6 53	..	7 22	7 57	8 27	8 53	9 28	..	9 53	1028	1053	..	..	7 37	..	7 57	..	8 15	8 54	..	9 24	9 53
Beddington Lane Halt	2 22	2 42	3 2	3 25	....	3 55	....	4 25	4 53	5 25	....	5 52	6 25	6 55	....	7 24	7 59	8 29	8 55	9 30	....	9 55	1030	1055	....	....	7 39	....	7 59	....	8 17	8 56	....	9 26	9 55
Waddon Marsh Halt	2 25	2 45	3 5	3 28	..	3 58	..	4 28	4 56	5 28	..	5 55	6 28	6 58	..	7 27	8 2	8 32	8 58	9 33	..	9 58	1033	1058	..	..	7 42	..	8 2	..	8 22	8 59	..	9 29	9 58
West Croydon arr	2 29	2 49	3 9	3 32	....	4 2	....	4 32	4 59	5 32	....	5 59	6 32	7 2	....	7 31	8 5	8 36	9 2	9 37	....	10 2	1037	11 2	....	....	7 45	....	8 6	....	8 26	9 2	....	9 32	10 2

For TRAINS between West Croydon and Wimbledon, via Sutton, see Table 68

573

Bradshaw's Timetable of 1956.

Sources and Acknowledgements

The following main sources have been used:

Bradshaw
Timetables of SR and BR(S)
Various articles, mainly in the *Railway Magazine*
Clinker's Register of Closed Passenger Stations (Avon-Anglia 1978)
A Southern Region Chronology and Record R.H. Clark (Oakwood Press 1964; and 1975 Suppt)
The Railway Clearing House Official Handbook of Railway Stations

Thanks are also due for help from the following members of the Transport Ticket Society: J. Britton, J. Shelbourn, J.B. Horne, L.M. Bell; also H.C. Casserley and H.V. Borley.

Dunsbear Halt. *Lens of Sutton*